NO.1 FALL 1996

NEW DIRECTIONS FOR SCHOOL LEADERSHIP

Every
Teacher
as a
Leader

Realizing the Potential of Teacher Leadership

RICHARD H. ACKERMAN
University of Massachusetts Lowell
Harvard Graduate School of Education
EDITOR-IN-CHIEF

GAYLE MOLLER
South Florida Center for Educational Leaders

MARILYN KATZENMEYER
West Central Educational Leadership Network
EDITORS

EVERY TEACHER AS A LEADER: REALIZING THE POTENTIAL OF TEACHER LEADERSHIP
Gayle Moller, Marilyn Katzenmeyer (eds.)
New Directions for School Leadership, No. 1, Fall 1996
Richard H. Ackerman, Editor-in-Chief

Microfilm copies of issues and articles are available in 16 mm and 35 mm, as well as microfiche in 105 mm, through University Microfilms Inc., 300 North Zeeb Road, Ann Arbor, Michigan 48106–1346.

ISSN 1089–5612   ISBN 0–7879–9861–3

NEW DIRECTIONS FOR SCHOOL LEADERSHIP is part of The Jossey-Bass Education Series and is published quarterly by Jossey-Bass Inc., Publishers, 350 Sansome Street, San Francisco, California 94104–1342.

SUBSCRIPTIONS: Please see Ordering Information on p. iv.
EDITORIAL CORRESPONDENCE should be sent to Richard Ackerman, The Principals' Center, Harvard Graduate School of Education, 336 Gutman Library, Cambridge, MA, 02138.

Manufactured in the United States of America on Lyons Falls Pathfinder Tradebook. This paper is acid-free and 100 percent totally chlorine-free.

The International Network of Principals' Centers

The International Network of Principals' Centers sponsors *New Directions for School Leadership* as part of its commitment to strengthening leadership at the individual school level through professional development for leaders. The Network has a membership of principals' centers, academics, and practitioners in the United States and overseas and is open to all groups and institutions committed to the growth of school leaders and the improvement of schools. The Network currently functions primarily as an information exchange and support system for member centers in their efforts to work directly with school leaders in their communities. Its office is in the Principals' Center at the Harvard Graduate School of Education.

The Network offers these services:

- The International Directory of Principals' Centers features member centers with contact persons, descriptions of center activities, program references, and evaluation instruments.
- The Annual Conversation takes place every spring, when members meet for seminars, workshops, speakers, and to initiate discussions that will continue throughout the year.
- *Newsnotes*, the Network's quarterly newsletter, informs members of programs, conferences, workshops, and special interest items.
- *Reflections*, an annual journal, includes articles by principals, staff developers, university educators, and principals' center staff members.

For further information, please contact:

International Network of Principals' Centers
Harvard Graduate School of Education
336 Gutman Library
Cambridge, MA 02138
(617) 495–9812

Ordering Information

NEW DIRECTIONS FOR SCHOOL LEADERSHIP
This series of paperback books provides principals, superintendents, teachers, and others who exercise leadership at the local level with insight and guidance on the important issues influencing schools and school leadership. Books in the series are published quarterly in Fall, Winter, Spring and Summer and are available for purchase both by subscription and individually.

SUBSCRIPTIONS for 1996–1997 cost $52.00 for individuals (a savings of 35 percent over single-copy prices) and $96.00 for libraries. There are no shipping and handling charges on subscriptions.

SINGLE COPIES cost $20.00 plus shipping. There will be handling charges on billed orders. Call the 800 number below for more information.

SINGLE COPIES AVAILABLE FOR SALE

SL1   Every Teacher as a Leader: Realizing the Potential of Teacher Leadership, *Gayle Moller, Marilyn Katzenmeyer*

QUANTITY DISCOUNTS ARE AVAILABLE. Please contact Jossey-Bass Periodicals for information at 1–415–433–1740.

TO ORDER, CALL 1–800–956–7739 or 1–415–433–1767
. . . and visit our website at http://www.josseybass.com

Contents

Teacher leadership, described throughout this volume, may be purposefully cultivated, or it may grow out of unanticipated circumstances. To take full advantage of this resource, the inevitable obstacles to teacher leadership must be addressed. With all stakeholders working together, these obstacles can be overcome, and we can tap the talents of the multitude of teachers who can, through their leadership, influence others toward improved practice.

1

The promise of teacher leadership

Gayle Moller, Marilyn Katzenmeyer

DURING THE LAST TEN YEARS, school reform has nudged teachers into leadership roles. In some schools the norm of isolation is being challenged by certain teachers, and these teachers are encouraging others to reconsider their instructional practices. Schools that have taken advantage of the valuable resource these teachers represent have seen the difference it can make. Students learn more, teachers are more satisfied with their work, and schools benefit from increased human capital.

The emergence of teacher leadership can be traced to three catalysts. First, teachers have engaged in new ways of teaching. These innovative methods may be related to a content area, such as process writing, or an instructional strategy, like cooperative

NEW DIRECTIONS FOR SCHOOL LEADERSHIP, NO. 1, FALL 1996 © JOSSEY-BASS PUBLISHERS

learning. As teachers gained confidence in their newly learned skills, they shared them. Other teachers listened; they came into these teacher leaders' classrooms and walked away with different ideas for their students. Credible teachers are influential with their colleagues—this powerful teacher leadership model has always existed in our schools. But the use of new strategies based on research has offered teacher leaders a legitimate avenue to open professional conversations with their peers.

Second, the widespread use of site-based decision making for school improvement has spurred the development of teacher leaders. Most states encourage (or require) a collaborative approach to planning for school goals. Although the principal, parents, and community leaders are represented in decision-making teams, the teachers are the ones who must execute the proposed plans. Recognizing their important influence on this process, teachers emerge as leaders of it. They may serve in formal positions (such as chairperson) on these teams, or they may remain informal leaders who can positively (or negatively) influence the actual work of school improvement. Previously teachers focused primarily on their own classroom; now they experience all the benefits and frustrations of working with other adults to improve their schools.

Finally, teacher leadership has emerged from teachers' involvement in networks or consortia of like-minded schools. For example, the Coalition of Essential Schools encourages teacher leadership through study groups, national symposiums, and other activities that honor teacher leadership. As teachers begin to share across school boundaries, they realize how much they have to offer one another. They begin to take responsibility for the success of projects rather than depend on administrators to be the sole providers of leadership. The relationships forged through these loose associations offer teachers a chance to accept the level of leadership that is comfortable for them. As they share with teachers in other schools, they realize that they are not the only ones committed to making a difference.

Four popular fallacies concerning teacher leadership

Teachers are beginning to see the value of sharing with one another. The appearance of teachers' study groups in schools is evidence of their wanting to learn together. Yet there is a side to our schools that inhibits such collegial experiences. There are obstacles that keep teacher leadership from reaching its full potential. In this chapter we examine four beliefs or feelings among teachers that pose obstacles to teacher leadership, and propose ways to overcome them:

1. *"I wouldn't call myself a leader."* At a national conference, two teachers were asked, "Are you interested in teacher leadership?" The teachers looked at each other, simultaneously pointed to their chests, and looked back with frowns. "Who me? No way," was one teacher's response. In further conversation, these two teachers revealed that they served on their district's professional development committee—they were, in fact, already teacher leaders. This simple example illustrates how teachers commonly do not see themselves as leaders.

Another example of a teacher who lacked awareness of her influence as a leader is Susan, a media specialist in a K–8 school. Susan is not only a leader in her school, she is also part of a cadre of teacher leaders across her state. One day Susan met with her school district's superintendent to persuade him to allow a teachers' guild to form. After the meeting, Susan shared, "I wouldn't call myself a teacher leader. Most of the teachers in our school would say Mary [the school's union steward] is a teacher leader." Teachers like these are leaders but do not see themselves this way or are reluctant to describe their work as leadership.

Why is it so difficult for teachers to acknowledge themselves as teacher leaders? Teachers are socialized to be followers, not leaders. Early in their development, they follow the lead of other, more experienced educators. Student teachers in undergraduate programs are observed and evaluated by university supervisors, principals, and cooperating teachers. These others, who are perceived to be leaders, are assigned to guide and direct the novice teacher. Only recently have university education programs begun to prepare student teachers to reflect on their practice and adjust it using their own knowledge and experience.

Policymakers also contribute to the socialization of teachers as followers. They assume that teachers need policies to tell them what is appropriate content at a certain grade level; this does little to encourage individual teachers to be leaders. The idea of allowing waivers to such policies, while a positive step toward freeing teachers from bureaucratic constraints that hinder their leadership, is nevertheless a symptom of the belief that someone in a leadership role outside the school has more expertise and wisdom than teachers themselves.

Forced into a managerial role in many districts, school principals reinforce the idea of teachers as followers. Teachers are monitored to ensure that specific tasks are completed on time and in the right way; priority is placed on paperwork and accurate reporting to the district office. Creative actions by teachers may require permission from the principal, and some teachers hesitate to go to all the trouble necessary to try something new. Principals who were themselves educated and socialized to expect a power-centered role may be unable to practice in ways that support teacher leadership (Hart and Murphy, 1994).

In hierarchically structured schools, *leader* tends to be synonymous with *boss*. Relationships between teachers and administrators are based on long-standing patterns and beliefs that reinforce the hierarchy. Further, some teachers view formal leadership positions with disdain and prefer to remain close to their students; thus it is understandable that teachers are reluctant to accept the title of "teacher leader" when it may be construed as an administrative role by their peers.

Teachers' reluctance to lead and to acknowledge themselves as leaders stems from two factors. First, past experiences in their school may not have encouraged teachers to take the risks necessary to lead. Also, confusion about what teacher leadership is causes teachers to shy away from identifying themselves as leaders.

The lack of a clear definition of teacher leadership also impedes its development. Defining this concept can lead to conversations that build a common understanding. Our definition of teacher leadership proposes that teachers are leaders when they are contributing to school reform or student learning (within or beyond the classroom), influencing others to improve their professional practice, or identifying with and contributing to a community of leaders (Katzenmeyer and Moller, 1996). When teachers measure their work against this definition, many realize that they are indeed teacher leaders, and others realize that they can be.

First, as competent professionals, teachers lead students in their learning. But once teachers gain mastery in their work with students, they can also reach beyond the classroom, to interact with other adults in the school community. For example, a first-grade teacher in a large school district is invited to facilitate the development of a vision statement at a districtwide meeting: this is teacher leadership in action. By becoming involved in school improvement projects, teachers can extend their influence within the school and also into the larger community.

Moving beyond the classroom to influence others is a leadership responsibility, and teachers are in the best position to do this. Teachers listen to other teachers—especially respected ones, for it is difficult to deny their ideas. This illustrates how teacher leadership supports improved practice. One high school teacher leader took on the onerous task of convincing her colleagues to honor more students, besides the traditional valedictorian and salutatorian, at graduation. Her colleagues agreed and decided to recognize the talents of graduating students that went beyond only grade point averages.

Finally, teacher leaders are not satisfied to work alone; they are anxious to engage with others in a community of leaders. The feelings of isolation experienced in the classroom can be the impetus for teachers to move beyond their classroom to work with other adults. One fifth-grade teacher described how she met informally with team members at lunch, despite their lack of free time, to "foster unity and dispel some rumors." This teacher builds her own community of leaders.

Encouraging teachers to accept the concept of teacher leadership should be handled with care. The notion of a single leader (the principal) is ingrained within the culture of schools, and this new perspective may be foreign to most teachers. Small discussion groups can be established to examine how teachers are leaders already. Once they look at leadership in this way, the label *leader* is no longer threatening. Recognizing teachers' leadership accomplishments in ways that are acceptable to them can help them become comfortable with a new definition of leadership.

Perhaps the most intimidating aspect of teacher leadership is the expectation that one will be asked to take on leadership tasks one fears. Teacher leadership entails a continuum of functions that may include both formal and informal roles. When asked about teacher leaders, most people have traditionally thought of formal positions such as department chairperson or team leader. Even the current research on teacher leadership is primarily focused on those obvious, formal leadership roles (Smylie, 1995). Teachers perform many other leadership tasks informally, however. And informal leadership roles, although they are more difficult to define, are usually more influential than formal roles. One principal has a list of leadership functions developed by the school improvement team. Each year teachers are invited to assume roles that appeal to them. Teacher leadership may range from helping a colleague in a one-on-one relationship to serving as a change agent for an entire school or beyond, to influence other schools.

If we are to enlist every teacher as a leader, then understanding the definition of teacher leadership is crucial to drawing attention to an assortment of teacher leadership functions, both formal and informal. Identifying yourself as a teacher leader is the first step to believing that you can influence others to improve teaching and learning. The belief that a teacher can take on leadership responsibilities without moving into an administrative or other formal position is critical as schools make teacher leadership a reality. We cannot assume that teachers see themselves as leaders. Developing teachers' awareness is the key to their accepting teacher leadership roles.

Once teachers accept their work as leadership, the context in which they work is a major concern. Even the most able teachers find it difficult to exert influence within a school that does not provide the resources or encouragement for teacher leadership. Not only do teachers need to feel comfortable with the definition, the principal's understanding of the potential of teacher leadership can determine how effective it can be in a school.

2.   *"It's a social indiscretion to share professional beliefs."* Teacher leaders know the trade-offs they must make when they decide to become leaders. The norms of the teaching profession do not encourage them to draw attention to themselves by agreeing to do additional tasks beyond those of a traditional classroom teacher. The reward for accepting leadership responsibilities may be the contempt of other teachers, who see this behavior as threatening to their own status. An example is the scorn that many teachers seeking national certification receive from their peers (Bradley, 1995). Loss of collegiality is painful, and it can persuade teachers to retreat into their classrooms and not participate in leadership activities. Each school's culture directly influences how willing its teachers will be to take on positive teacher leadership roles.

Teachers must be willing to risk rejection from their peers when they become leaders. Teacher leadership is inconsistent with the egalitarian culture in most schools. The norm is for all teachers to work under the same rules and with equal compensation. Hart (1995) suggests that this egalitarianism is antithetical to the flexibility and dispersed expertise needed if teachers are to lead instructional and curriculum reform. The opinions of peers are important to teachers, and negative comments about accepting leadership roles may stop their initiatives. Members of negative cliques can be powerful forces, placing roadblocks in the way of teacher leadership.

Teachers' lounges are notorious for their lack of positive professional exchanges. Teachers who try to change this situation are placing themselves in harm's way. Rosenholtz's work on teacher uncertainty and self-esteem (1989) helps explain why teachers avoid talking about their practice. Teachers' uncertainty is based on our own feelings of inadequacy in the teaching process. Teachers may believe that their success in the classroom is due to chance rather than their knowledge of the teaching craft. So when students fail, the conversation centers on the students' inadequacies, in order to maintain teachers' self-esteem. How many teachers would tell their peers that chance and a personal lack of skill are the basis of their practice?

Moving beyond the classroom is risky. Teacher isolation is the norm; teachers do not expect to share their practice with one another. This expectation of privacy within teaching (Little, 1989) ultimately inhibits teachers from extending their influence beyond their classroom doors. It is difficult enough to try to influence your peers when you have the school community's support; when the school culture ridicules this type of behavior, it is unlikely that you will even try. Fortunately, teachers now have a reason to move beyond the "no sharing" rule. This reason is the complexity they face when using innovative strategies in order to reach all students.

Teachers in schools with a collaborative culture open to teacher leadership find that there are many opportunities to help one another. In this type of school teachers move in and out of one another's classrooms, helping colleagues who are having problems. They accept professional talk as essential to their growth and development. In schools where collaboration is the exception, teachers rarely know what is going on in the classroom right next door (Heller and Firestone, 1995). They may assume that all is well, but on what basis? These types of schools are like health clubs where large numbers of people come to get fit but few speak to one another, except to exchange superficial pleasantries. Sometimes they share their strategies for getting fit, but most of the time they struggle alone. Teaching can be similar.

If teachers want to be leaders and their school community celebrates the value of teacher leadership, then the door is open to provide professional development that enhances teachers' efforts. Recognizing that teachers can learn through a variety of strategies, there must be a conscious effort to make it happen.

3. *"Teacher leaders are born, not made."* The literature abounds with stories that illustrate the importance of providing professional development experiences for potential and practicing administrators. Graduate programs, school district staff development, and training seminars all offer these school leaders opportunities for becoming more skillful. There are few examples of programs—at the college or university level, in school districts, or as part of staff development—that address teacher leadership, however. If school administrators need leadership development, why not teacher leaders? As Goodlad (1990) points out, "There is irresponsibility in significantly expanding teachers' authority without educating them to use it well" (p. 27).

In schools that recognize the value of building this resource, teacher leaders are offered opportunities to develop. Often the principals in these schools are promoting significant change themselves, and they are not doing it alone. They are quick to recognize and promote partnerships with teacher leaders. Teachers are invited to participate in professional development activities, to visit other schools, and to be involved in significant decision making within the school. Once a teacher shows an interest in an area, these principals quickly secure resources to support this interest.

Professional development for teacher leaders may be formal or informal. Formal work may include workshops, conferences, or study groups. Informal learning takes place when teachers visit one another's classrooms, read a book related to their interest, or spend time studying with other teachers. Whatever the avenue of learning, the most meaningful experiences are those that relate directly to teachers' perceived needs.

Too often, "experts" are enlisted to tell teachers what they need to do to improve their teaching and learning. Instead, teachers can be invited to invent their own solutions to problems within their school rather than to depend on someone else to prescribe solutions. There can be a balance between redefining the experts as the people who do the work and learning from others whose experiences can inform teachers' practice.

Several professional development programs we offer to teacher leaders try to strike that balance. It is crucial to give teacher leaders adequate time to sort through their own beliefs, examine new ideas, and determine the gaps between the two. Then teachers can make sense of how this might influence their work in their own context (Little, 1993). Although it is important to review the research on improved teaching and learning, unless teacher leaders can make their own meaning out of this information, their new leadership behavior may be extinguished when they reenter the classroom. It takes time for reflection to integrate research with practice.

Time is a valuable commodity in schools. Teachers are expected to be in contact with students all day, every day. When teacher leaders are instead allowed the time they need to work through issues and to make sense out of school reform, the payoff in the long term is well worth it. In one of our leadership programs, teachers and other educators work together over a six-month period to examine how change takes place in schools and to build their skills to work with others through the change process. Most educators enter the program with preconceived ideas about "how to change others." By the end of the program, these same people speak about how they personally must change before they can work with others (Saxl and Lewandowski, 1995).

Teachers who are treated with respect and offered a chance to examine their own values and beliefs rise to the occasion and lead positive change in their work with colleagues. Seldom do we meet teachers in our programs, whatever their level of leadership in their school, who do not recognize how they can make a difference in their schools. This cannot be accomplished during a two-hour meeting after teaching all day, in three-hour seminars, or even in self-directed study. The type of behavior change necessary requires an ongoing interaction with other colleagues in a risk-free environment.

Professional development then becomes a continuous learning experience for teacher leaders. The principal can support this by seeking out these types of experiences. Actual involvement of the principal with teacher leaders in professional development reinforces the value placed on learning in the school. If the principal engages with the teachers as a colearner, outcomes can be even further enhanced. One principal who attends conferences with her teacher leaders purposely plans social events on these trips. This might include a baseball game, a visit to a local attraction, or even a game of billiards. These teachers know that their learning is important, because the principal takes the time to be a learner with them, both formally and informally.

4.   *"It's my own responsibility to make myself into a leader."* The promise of teacher leadership cannot be accomplished without a belief among educators and other stakeholders that leadership development is a shared responsibility. If efforts were initiated on a widespread basis—if the goal of preparing all teachers as leaders were systematically pursued by colleges and universities, principals, district staff members, and teachers themselves—then teacher leadership would not be a novel idea. It would be expected of all teachers.

What can be done to develop teacher leaders

Colleges and universities

Colleges and universities can begin the work of preparing teachers as leaders early in teachers' development. The challenge for universities is to expose their undergraduate education students to the potential of schools in the future and to emphasize that leadership is an appropriate role for all teachers. As schools continue to reform, leadership will become a critical competency for every teacher.

As education students move into the observation phase of their program, colleges and universities should expect that in addition to classroom experiences they will observe school governance groups, participate in team planning events, and become acquainted with the effective adult interactions that are so crucial to success in today's schools. Beginning teachers will need to enter the profession with the skills needed to be team members, to use collaborative decision-making processes, and to be confident managing conflict. Educational leadership programs have traditionally prepared individuals to lead entire schools or districts; perhaps it is time to reconsider whether these programs should be adapted to prepare teachers to be leaders as well (see Chapter Eight). Several initiatives to provide graduate education in teacher leadership are currently in place around the country.

Principals

Teacher leaders' effectiveness depends not only on their own commitment to be leaders but also on the ability of their school's principal to skillfully support them and encourage a culture that allows teacher leadership to exist. Here is where principals' leadership is crucial. Regardless of the beliefs principals espouse, unless structures are established to encourage teacher leadership, there will be only a token use of this valuable resource.

In the current structure of schools, the principal is the most important person to affect the willingness of the school community to accept teacher leaders. If they are viewed as threats to the formal power structure or if leadership is restricted to the talents of a few teachers given formal leadership assignments, then the school suffers. On the other hand, in schools where teacher leadership is welcomed, the principal benefits. To capitalize on this resource, principals must effectively manage relationships, find time to offer frequent encouragement, and identify appropriate recognition.

Relationships between the principal and teachers in the school can enhance or detract from teacher leadership. The complexity of principal-teacher relationships is the product of the typical hierarchical structure in schools. A middle school principal shared how he was appointed directly to the principalship in a school where he was previously a teacher leader. Immediately, collaboration was strained with colleagues he had taught with as peers, making for a difficult transition. Principals walk tightropes in maintaining collegial atmospheres (for example, sometimes they are unable to share confidential information that may influence their decisions). Even the most well-meaning principal can find it a challenge to maintain positive relationships within his or her school.

Rather than relying on only a few teachers, administrators can distribute the workload more evenly and involve more teachers. When every teacher is invited to be a leader and is asked to take on leadership roles based on their areas of interest, then those teachers who rise to the occasion will more likely be supported by their colleagues. This places a heavy burden on the principal to spend quality time in classrooms, around the building, and in areas where teachers congregate. During this time out of the office, the principal becomes a detective, looking for credible, effective teachers and encouraging them to pursue their passions in education. The teachers' interests may be a formal program, like an approach to mathematics, or it may be a leadership role that influences decisions within the school. Regardless of their area of interest, however, there is always a need for ongoing support and encouragement (including the necessary resources). The managerial tasks of the principalship must take a back seat to the important role of developing teacher leaders.

Rewarding those teachers who are willing to move beyond their classrooms to lead others is a complicated issue. Groups of educators who discuss teacher leadership frequently focus on monetary rewards. The debate begins with comparisons to athletic coaches and other teachers who take on extra tasks for an additional stipend. This approach has not had encouraging results with teacher leaders, however. In a follow-up study of trained teacher leaders, principals reported three ways in which they were able to provide real support and incentives for teachers engaged in both classroom teaching and teacher leadership responsibilities. First, the principals provided access to information and resources and gave their personal time to support the teacher leaders. Second, they honored teacher leaders' requests for professional development and sometimes initiated opportunities for them to attend conferences or represent the school at important meetings. Finally, they gave them the gift of time, covering classes for them, providing substitute teachers, or assigning support personnel to assist them (Hart, Lewandowski, Segesta, and Bane, 1995).

If the only rewards of teacher leadership are additional responsibilities, teachers may be discouraged from making further efforts. Rather than rewarding the efforts of outstanding teachers, the practice in education is simply to expect more work. As one teacher said, "She [the principal] pats me on the back, and then I get another job." Teachers are initially enthusiastic about leadership roles and gladly accept more responsibility. But if the only reward is more work, teachers will see the pattern and decline future leadership roles. The worst scenario is when teachers, who are already overloaded, try to achieve both in their classrooms and in leadership roles. The outcome for such teachers can be anger, burnout, or a decline in performance.

Any change in the egalitarian norms of teachers will place pressure for change on principals, district staff, and other teachers. In this sourcebook, Kahrs (Chapter Two) recommends several practices that he has found to be successful in implementing the teacher-as-leader concept at the high school level, and Boles and Troen (Chapter Three) describe the importance of principals' encouragement in professional development schools. Both chapters provide insights into the efforts principals can make to begin to develop teacher leadership.

District staff

To support the development of teachers as leaders, district staff can begin shifting from "doing" to "enabling others to do." Rather than writing curriculum guides that teachers ignore, enlightened district staff develop the capacity of teacher teams to prepare curriculum and instructional strategies that are consistent with state and district goals yet are designed to meet the needs of individual schools. Rather than delivering staff development programs themselves or bringing in experts, they can develop teachers' capacity to lead study groups, or create opportunities for teachers to share the expertise they have gained in their classrooms with colleagues through presentations, mentoring, or peer coaching (see Chapter Four).

The role of district staff is also critical in supporting the development of teacher leadership. Fullan (1993) reminds us that both bottom-up and top-down efforts are needed to make real progress with school change. District staff assist teacher leaders from the top of the organization. For example, examinations by district staff of policies that may stand in the way of teacher leadership practices further the cause of teacher leadership. Principals can be released from constraining norms that inhibit change, such as hiring practices that restrict teacher involvement in selecting competent colleagues. Principals who are empowered by their district and provided with more leeway in making changes are more able to empower their teachers.

Teachers

Teachers themselves can advance teacher leadership efforts in their schools. The first responsibility is for teachers to focus on their own personal awareness. What strengths can they bring to teacher leadership tasks? What skills and knowledge do they need to develop to be effective leaders? Individual teachers can consider how willing they are to take on the risk of becoming a leader, since currently it is the individual teacher's prerogative to accept or decline the role of teacher leader.

Teachers who wish to see teacher leadership thrive have an obligation to begin developing positive and collaborative relationships with other faculty and staff members. Opening the classroom door, encouraging colleagues to share, and participating with others on teams, committees, and task forces are all ways to shape collegial school environments. Developing positive relationships requires effective listening and communicating, and valuing and appreciating one another's differences. The effectiveness of social relationships in schools can pave the way for teacher leadership or hinder it from evolving.

Building a critical mass of teacher leaders within a school can relieve the dependence on a single, charismatic principal for leadership. One teacher leader shared this lesson: "I used to think that the principal was the most important person in the building. The kind of school I worked at was based on my principal. I now know that a school can have the best principal, but if the school has poor teachers, nothing will change. Teachers are the most important factor in the building. For a school to be successful, the teachers are the ones who make the difference, not the principal. Teachers can change, improve, or kill a program."

Conclusion

Teacher leadership is a resource for changing schools. Using the knowledge, skills, and talents of every teacher as a leader provides unlimited resources for positive outcomes. The obstacles discussed here to the widespread institutionalization of teacher leadership are a reality in many schools and districts across the country. The act of defining them and beginning to devote our collective energies to inventing strategies to overcome them provides hope that the future promise of teacher leadership may be achieved. Teachers themselves, principals, district staff, and colleges and universities all share a responsibility for developing teachers as leaders. Our students will be the winners if we resolve these issues and encourage teachers to be leaders in our schools.

References

Bradley, A. "What Price Success?" *Education Week*, 1995, *15*(12), 1, 8.

Fullan, M. *Change Forces*. New York: Falmer Press, 1993.

Goodlad, J. "The Occupation of Teaching in Schools." In J. Goodlad, R. Soder, and K. Sirotnik (eds.), *The Moral Dimensions of Teaching*. San Francisco: Jossey-Bass, 1990.

Hart, A. W. "Reconceiving School Leadership: Emergent View." *The Elementary School Journal*, 1995, *96*(1), 9–28.

Hart, A. W., and Murphy, M. J. "Preparing Principals to Lead in Restructured Schools." In P. Thurston and N. Prestine (eds.), *Advances in Educational Administration*. Greenwich, Conn.: JAI Press, 1994.

Hart, P., Lewandowski, A., Segesta, J., and Bane, M. *Evaluation of Leadership Development for Teachers*. Tampa, Fla.: West Central Educational Leadership Network, 1995.

Heller, M. F., and Firestone, W. A. "Who's in Charge Here? Sources of Leadership for Change in Eight Schools." *The Elementary School Journal*, 1995, *96*(1), 65–86.

Katzenmeyer, M., and Moller, G. *Awakening the Sleeping Giant: Leadership Development for Teachers.* Thousand Oaks, Calif.: Corwin Press, 1996.

Little, J. W. "The Persistence of Privacy: Autonomy and Initiative in Teachers' Professional Relations." Paper presented at the annual meeting of the American Educational Research Association, San Francisco, March 1989.

Little, J. W. *Teachers' Professional Development in a Climate of Educational Reform.* New York: National Center for Restructuring Education, Schools, and Teaching, 1993.

Rosenholtz, S. J. *Teachers' Workplace: The Social Organization of Schools.* New York: Longman, 1989.

Saxl, E., and Lewandowski, A. *Florida Assisting Change in Education: A Research and Evaluation Study.* Davie, Fla.: South Florida Center for Educational Leaders, 1995.

Smylie, M. "New Perspectives on Teacher Leadership." *The Elementary School Journal,* 1995, *96*(1), 3–7.

GAYLE MOLLER *is director of the South Florida Center for Educational Leaders in Davie, Florida.*

MARILYN KATZENMEYER *is director of the West Central Educational Leadership Network in Tampa, Florida.*

This chapter defines what principals actually do to support teacher leadership. The author, a high school principal, shares how his experiences affect the support he gives teacher leaders in his school. The author initiated a five-year program for the professional development of teacher leaders in his school, using a shared governance approach. He explains actions he took in three areas: readiness for change, use of time, and development of school culture. Specific recommendations for practice at the school site are offered.

2

Principals who support teacher leadership

James R. Kahrs

OVER THE PAST TWELVE YEARS, since *A Nation at Risk*, teachers have been asked to accomplish more with students at all grade levels. In response, many attempts have been made to reinvent or reform education. Standards have been raised in nearly every state, yet we continue to hear about the "failure" of our public schools. As a high school principal for eleven of the past seventeen years, I have used a number of strategies for developing teachers as leaders. I have found ways to incorporate change into the daily routine of teaching and to help teachers find renewed enthusiasm, despite the external pressures placed on them. Such measures are more important than ever. As Barth (1990) says, "those who value public education, those who hope to improve our schools, should be worried about the stunted growth of teachers" (p. 49).

NEW DIRECTIONS FOR SCHOOL LEADERSHIP, NO. 1, FALL 1996 © JOSSEY-BASS PUBLISHERS

I am convinced that change in our schools can only come about as a result of teacher leadership, with principals' support. The role of dynamic leadership is worth sharing with all who frequent the schoolhouse. My vision is to provide an environment where all employees are free to lead and learn, where power is attained by group involvement and empowerment, and where success is measured by the quality and quantity of leadership a school displays. Developing teachers as leaders can only be accomplished through the process of empowerment in the schools.

Empowerment is a term that has many meanings to different educational stakeholders. The definition I adopt reflects my personal belief as a principal about the potential of empowered teachers to change schools. Starratt (1995) suggests, "Empowerment is not a process of administrators' giving power to teachers. Rather, it is a process that involves mutual respect, dialogue, and invitation; it implies recognition that each person enjoys talents, competencies, and potentials that can be exercised in responsible and creative ways within the school setting for the benefit of children and youth" (p. 42). In my experience, empowerment of teachers as leaders holds great potential for reforming schools. Empowering teachers gives the principal an opportunity to develop his or her vision and to share his or her work with the teachers who are most concerned about students' success.

It seems to me that the brightest glimmer of hope on the horizon for public education is to make the individual school the locus of control for the development of teacher leadership. Site-based management can provide a real means for initiating change at the school level, utilizing a process of shared governance that is developed and followed by the local schools. As I consider site-based management, I believe that local schools must have control of their own resources as well as accountability for their students' achievement. Shared governance requires a real sense of democratic decision making that is endorsed and supported by the administration, and it is essential that the principal "walk the talk." To this end the school needs to develop a constitution and by-laws that are endorsed by the principal and approved by the board of education. Schlechty (1990), a leader in school reform, supports this form of democratic governance in schools: "Participatory leadership makes sense in school because this pattern of leadership promises to yield better decisions and better results" (p. 52).

Though governance may take many shapes, the principles of "one principal, one vote" and "no veto" seem to be tenets that are at the heart of shared governance in schools. Effective shared governance encourages an environment in which teachers can become empowered and develop as leaders. In the next few pages I will share some of my experiences and what I have found to be successful in facilitating shared governance and teacher leadership in the high school setting.

First, I describe my own history as an educator and the experiences that influence my thinking and practice today as a principal. Second, I share three main themes that have guided my work: readiness for change, the use of time, and the development of school culture. Finally, in making recommendations for practice, I explain formal and informal structures that work for me.

My experience developing teacher leaders

Like so many others, my focus as a beginning teacher during the mid 1970s was personal survival. But as my career progressed and I became comfortable with my teaching, I began to look beyond my own classroom and students. I became concerned about improving the basic operations of the school. As a result of faculty discontent over the discipline and attendance procedures at the school where I taught, a faculty council was developed to discuss problems, formulate committees, and present possible solutions to the administration. The council was an advisory body to the principal; he maintained the power to make decisions. I worked on committees to develop new and better procedures based on tougher, more rigid discipline models. It was my experience that the council's recommendations tended to focus on the work of others, especially administrators, and on issues that had little impact on teaching and learning. I began to see that the "new and better" procedures had already been tried, over and over, and that the tougher, more rigid models resulted in students and teachers who followed directions but lacked creativity and deep involvement in the educational process. The process demonstrated to me the potential power of collective decision making, however. As I learned about shared decision making, I realized that the process needed to be expanded to involve decisions that had a direct effect on the real work of teaching and learning in the school. It was not effective, it seemed to me, to engage teachers in decision making that was not directly relevant to their roles. I recognized that if schools involved teachers in making decisions only about issues such as student parking, fund-raising drives, or the cafeteria, we would never impact teaching and learning through shared governance processes.

In 1979 I became the principal of a rural secondary school on the eastern end of Long Island, New York. The community thrived on weekend tourism from New York City yuppies, but its farms were dying, and school enrollment was decreasing at a drastic rate. The teachers' union resisted any change, especially staff reductions. Innovative strategies were needed to deal with the problems resulting from a reduced workforce, low teacher and student morale, and a changing community. Teachers who were well respected in the community were being forced from their positions. Building on my experiences as a teacher involved in governance in an advisory capacity, I began to focus teacher leadership efforts in my school on student success. Teachers had real authority to make decisions in those areas. I came to believe that teachers should engage in governance activities that affect their work and have an impact on student learning. Issues concerning curricula, instructional strategies, grading, attendance, and scheduling are all relevant to student outcomes, and teachers should therefore be involved in making decisions that affect such matters. Teachers in our school were taking risks while they learned new skills as a result of being given control of their working and learning environment. As a result, teachers developed an expanded ability to make decisions, they got more involved in the school, and the school's climate began to improve significantly.

I moved to Georgia to complete my doctoral studies. Then I took a position as an assistant principal in a large suburban high school outside Atlanta. I found that despite the change from a rural high school in Long Island to a suburban school in Georgia, the issues and opportunities were very similar. Both schools were faced with the challenge of rapid change. This created some unique problems for each school, but solutions were achieved using very similar strategies. I had the opportunity to develop a shared governance organization within the high school that led not only to teacher involvement but also to teacher empowerment. My practice was guided by my involvement with Carl Glickman at the University of Georgia and the League of Professional Schools, a network of schools that promotes democratic governance focused on teaching and learning.

The outcomes we experienced at this suburban high school were very positive. Teacher-led projects resulted in measurable positive results that included increased learning, fewer discipline problems, and higher attendance. Teachers participated in gathering and analyzing data as they developed their skills as action researchers. They began to understand that the improved attendance and discipline was a result of improved student learning, which had come about because of teacher leadership and involvement. Data generated within the school drove the decisions we made; these action research strategies were initiated because of our work with the League. Teachers' roles evolved from action researcher to continuing learner and, ultimately, teacher leader. After serving for three years as an assistant principal, I accepted the principalship of a high school about seventy miles from Atlanta. I began this principalship with a vision of incorporating many of the solutions I had learned during my years in education. One of my first actions was to work with others to develop a mission. As a result of our work we adopted this mission for our school: "To serve our community by providing each student educational opportunities designed to ensure success as an involved and responsible citizen. We are committed to providing a safe and positive environment, recognizing and addressing individual differences, involving parents, and making wise use of community resources." I view my role as the guardian of the mission and the facilitator of teacher and student leadership.

Three main themes of my work

I set a five-year goal for myself that centered around a plan for the professional development of teachers as leaders in the context of shared governance. Applying the guiding rules of shared governance (Glickman, 1993), I provided opportunities for everyone to be involved in decision making. I was committed to keeping my attention and actions consistent with the five-year goals. Three main themes guided my work: readiness for change, the use of time, and the development of the school culture.

Readiness for change

Concepts from the literature, especially Glickman (1993) and Starratt (1995), shaped my thinking about how to begin to work with my faculty if I was serious about making change. I recognized that individuals within an organization have their own state of readiness for change and growth. They develop as teacher leaders at different rates and under different conditions. Glickman (1993) explains that teachers grow as a result of their individual characteristics as well as the influences of their work environment and the teaching profession. An individual teacher's development involves interactions among the teacher, his or her peers, and the principal. The principal can facilitate teacher readiness by working directly with teachers and altering the work environment to encourage change.

Teachers' growth is also influenced by the time available and the culture of the school. Starratt (1995) equates readiness with empowerment: "Empowerment has to happen with each individual teacher. Each teacher must be invited to be authentically herself or himself. Sometimes that invitation will be very direct. . . . Sometimes that invitation will be indirect. . . . Sometimes the invitation will simply be an attentive ear" (p. 42). It was not long before I began to try out my understanding of the concepts of readiness and empowerment. Involving several teachers in the hiring of a new assistant principal was the first step I took in a long process of developing the whole faculty's readiness for change.

Early in my tenure as a high school principal in Georgia, I needed to replace the assistant principal for instruction, who had been moved to another school. Rather than have the other assistant principals or central office personnel assist in the selection process, I enlisted the help of the English and science department chairpersons to interview applicants and make a recommendation to the superintendent of schools. I had no prior knowledge of any faculty members, so I selected these individuals simply because they were department leaders. After screening applications and extensive interviewing, we all agreed on a candidate and recommended her to the superintendent. Upon learning that she would not be released from a contract in another district, we began the process again. After much discussion and additional interviews, I wanted one person and they wanted another. I recommended their choice. It was clear to me that this was a risk, but I believed that their trust in the process and in my intentions to involve them in making decisions depended on my actions in this case. I modeled with these two individual teachers what I hoped to show the entire faculty. I believe that this one event was more pivotal to the future of shared governance and teacher leadership in our school than anyone could have predicted. Teachers observed how I involved the two department heads in selecting the assistant principal, and they began to recognize that participative decision making and teacher governance were really going to be a reality at our school. Just as a teacher develops, so does an entire faculty and staff. The state of readiness of a loosely coupled group of educators varies greatly from school to school. This was just a beginning, but my hope was that eventually the faculty would begin to look beyond the classroom and view the process of teaching and learning as a collective effort.

I found that, to continue to pave the way for developing faculty readiness for change, the principal must know the individual faculty members, what motivates them, what they like to do, what skills they possess, and their strengths and weaknesses. During the first year as principal, I concentrated my efforts on school management and on getting to know the faculty and staff as individuals. I learned their strengths and weaknesses by observing them, talking with them, and working with them.

Empowering teachers in schools is best accomplished by matching their strengths with student needs rather than by concentrating on their weaknesses. In order to provide such an environment, I helped our teachers to understand my belief that education is a people-centered profession and that teachers' families must come first. A teacher dealing with a family crisis cannot be effective in the classroom. When I become aware of a family problem, such as a sickness in the family or the death of a close friend or loved one, I make personal contact with the faculty or staff member so there is no misunderstanding about his or her ability to take the necessary time to see the crisis through. It is true that some will take advantage of a particular situation in order to benefit themselves, but I believe teachers are more dedicated to their students and their colleagues when they know there is support during a personal crisis. All teachers and staff members are more understanding of students and colleagues when they know they will be supported in similar situations.

In order to facilitate these teacher leadership concepts, the principal needs to continually face some tough issues. The principal is traditionally the head of the school and the person who makes all decisions of consequence to the operation of the school. Parents, central office personnel, community members, and boards of education believe that the principal is the primary decision maker. Although the school system's organizational chart makes it clear who is responsible for the school, the bylaws or principles of shared governance give the principal just one vote and no veto. The struggle is that the principal must retain the responsibility but be willing to give up the authority to others. To be responsible for one's school while letting others make the decisions is not a strategy to be taken lightly.

Just as the principal struggles with his or her role under shared governance, the role of the teacher must also be understood in relation to the issues of readiness, time, and culture. New and veteran teachers alike have the same view of how schools are and should be governed; they have had role models for it since they entered kindergarten. Teachers must be ready for new and different challenges, or a basic change in attitudes will not develop. In order to create an environment in which change is acceptable, teachers must be comfortable with their own abilities. They must see the need for change and realize that they can effect it. This readiness is not easily seen or evaluated, but it will emerge when the conditions become correct. The principal must set the stage for teacher leadership and allow teachers to seize the opportunity when they recognize the need. Setting the stage for teacher leadership involves more than developing a policy for shared governance. It involves a systematic, deliberate attempt on the part of the principal to provide a variety of opportunities and invitations that will entice teachers to view schooling from a different perspective. The principal must demonstrate to teachers, through direct action, that their leadership can make a difference in the operation of the school.

The faculty's readiness for change at my school has continued to evolve. The best evidence I have that we are now ready to move toward true shared leadership began last spring. As a result of the doubling of the cost of paper and our inability to purchase it in large quantities, we were forced to drastically cut back on our usage. A group of teachers approached me and asked if they could develop "challenge" groups to work on school-related issues. They began with the paper shortage. The groups were organized by the teachers, leaders were selected, and issues debated. The teachers developed a plan that reorganized the way they delivered instruction, and as a result paper consumption was dramatically reduced, copier costs decreased, and teacher leadership was enhanced. The challenge groups continue and are taking on new issues. After this success, I believe we have turned the corner on teachers' readiness to be leaders.

Use of time

The effective use of time is vital in implementing shared governance. School calendars and teacher work schedules are most often dictated by school system needs and teacher contracts. Everyone must understand that the use of a democratic governance process takes time and the commitment of all involved. Even simple decisions require discussion and deliberation. Faculty members often become frustrated with what appears to be a lack of progress when decisions take a long time.

Finding time for teacher leadership is essential if we are to accomplish the development of democratic decision making in the school context. In writing about school reform, Darling-Hammond (1993) tells us, "The new model of school reform must seek to develop communities of learning grounded in communities of democratic discourse. It is only in this way that communities can come to want for all their children what they would want for their most advantaged—an education for empowerment and an education for freedom" (p. 761). In an attempt to provide teachers with opportunities to lead, I try to provide an environment that is non-threatening, open, and supportive of change. Creating an environment where the teacher is always part of the solution, not part of the problem, is the goal I continue to work toward. To facilitate this, I must focus on using time creatively so that teachers can engage in this form of decision making.

This understanding—that time is a resource—has been critical in the development of programs for shared governance and teacher leadership at my school. It is essential that the principal find adequate time for teachers to take part in democratic decision making.

This time should be above and beyond what is required for teacher planning. I make sure department chairpersons have a common planning period so that weekly meetings can take place without loss of class time or individual planning time. The answers are more complex when teachers are asked to leave teaching time to deal with governance or staff development issues. A delicate balance must be maintained to ensure accountability in the classroom and participation in school and leadership activities.

Also, decision making takes longer when more people are involved. It is much more efficient for a few administrators to make all the decisions. Teachers are accustomed to quick decisions and timely problem solving, and they must adjust to the new and different conditions under shared decision making. Glickman (1993) states, "A school must strike a balance between the time people are willing to give to a schoolwide democratic process and the time individuals must devote to their classrooms, families, and personal affairs" (p. 134).

As teachers become leaders they use more and more time outside the classroom in order to affect the total school environment. One might argue that this increase in time spent on schoolwide issues would reduce their effectiveness in the classroom; however, there is evidence to support just the opposite. Barth (1990) cites literature on successful corporations (such as IBM) that have used participatory decision making in terms of production, quality of work, and satisfaction. He draws conclusions from their experience for teaching: "By sharing leadership, teachers will feel more ownership of the commitment to decisions. And by providing teachers with leadership opportunities, one accords them recognition. Therefore, they will work harder and better and longer. In short, research suggests that the greater the participation in decision making, the greater the productivity, job satisfaction, and organizational commitment" (p. 130).

Time is a subject of great importance to our faculty and staff. I have taken steps to use our time together to focus on issues that are schoolwide in nature. The leadership team planned our last work day at the end of a grading period. The agenda for that day was to include staff development activities dealing with the identification of students under the influence of controlled substances, as well as small group sessions dealing with the concerns of moving to a block schedule. These programs took four hours, or more than half the work day. A small group of teachers expressed concerns about getting grades and other work completed in the short period of time that remained. Their peers responded clearly and loudly that the staff development was necessary and essential to the progress of the school. Teachers are beginning to see the need for collective dialogue to solve problems and are taking leadership in the use of available time to facilitate that dialogue.

School culture

The concept of school culture is complex and important in the process of developing both teachers as leaders and shared governance. The culture of a school includes its history, beliefs, values, norms and standards, and patterns of behavior. In order for change to become institutionalized, it must become embedded in the school's culture. A change in policy is not always reflected in a change of practice. We have known for years that teachers close their doors and teach the curriculum they feel is most important, not necessarily what is in the curriculum guides. A change in culture takes time, patience, and determination. According to Sergiovanni and Starratt (1988, p. 103), "The concept of culture is very important, for its dimensions are much more likely to govern what it is that people think and do than is the official management system." My early learning about school culture came as a first-year principal in New York, when I attempted to change the time and structure of the school's annual open house. The changes were not radical, but they were viewed by the faculty as "not the way we do it here." The culture of this school had set traditions and teacher expectations for events beyond the school day. I learned quickly the power of culture and that although I had the administrative power to make changes, I did not have the power to change the school's culture or traditions without the support or leadership of the faculty.

Culore

...s as the school grows and

...system of beliefs begins

...becomes the respon-

...administrators to

...hing and learn-

...of the school

...cus on issues that

...sues that are personal

...one's car or when one has

...when the dialogue revolves

are... ...y experience has taught me that the p... ...such dialogue is critical in developing and i... ...ective culture.

As teache... ...more comfortable with being involved and expressing the... ...ves, the principal must be sure to pay attention to them and their ideas. Teachers must feel that they can express their opinions without fear of retribution. I have an open-door policy in my office, and I use annual evaluations of me by staff to keep my focus on the education of young adults. I report suggestions and criticisms to the leadership team and faculty (without using names). Recently I received a note from a teacher requesting that I reformat faculty meetings to incorporate teacher and department concerns early in the meeting rather than at the end of the meeting, when we always seem to run out of time. I made the change, and I appreciated that it was teacher-generated. All events such as parent meetings, open houses, and in-service days are followed by a written evaluation, and tools such as exam schedules and student and teacher handbooks are evaluated as well. Teachers and administrators review the evaluations and make changes for the future.

Teachers exercising leadership in the context of democratic decision making will have a drastic effect on the culture of their school, and that evolving culture will generate continued growth in the process of governance, creating new avenues for teacher leadership. To effectively change the culture of a school, leadership must exist at both the administrative level and the teacher level. Schlechty (1988) reinforces these ideas: "For change to occur, it is essential that those who are most directly affected by the change be involved both in defining the problem and in identifying the solution; even more important, they must perceive themselves as being involved" (p. 187).

To make this change in school culture, I have found that the principal is continually challenged to change his or her practices to fit the paradigm of sharing leadership with teachers. Maintaining a balance between leading and delegating requires constant attention. There is no clear guideline to determine the correct balance for any one principal. The idea or concept that leads to the decision must dictate the balance, and the underlying barometer must be what is in the best interest of students. Odden and Wohlstetter (1995) identify the principal of a school with school-based management as "one who can [both] lead and delegate. These principals [play] a key role in several areas: dispersing power, promoting a schoolwide commitment to growth in skills and knowledge, getting teachers to participate in the work of the school, collecting information about student learning, and distributing rewards. The principals [are] often described as facilitators and leaders, as strong supporters of their staffs, and as the people who [introduce] innovations and [move] the reform agenda forward" (p. 35).

As a principal struggling to maintain this balance, several specific insights about school culture change have guided my actions:

1. *Teacher-generated change is supported by encouragement and the allocation of resources.* We are currently in the process of moving to block scheduling for our high school. Teachers were instrumental in conceptualizing the change and are actively involved in researching the idea, visiting schools, and developing the new schedule. I have used the principal's account to support staff development, to fund site visits, and to purchase reference materials for this schoolwide effort.

2. *Administrative support for teachers must be apparent in the daily operation of the classroom.* No teacher should be placed in the position of having a student be disrespectful or insubordinate to him or her. This is not tolerated in our school, and admin-

istrators deal with student behavior problems quickly and appropriately when teachers request it.

3. *Recognition of leadership and credit for leadership among teachers is a key factor influencing continued teacher involvement and leadership.* At my school, a portion of each faculty meeting is set aside for recognizing faculty accomplishments, whether school-related or personal. Teachers of the month are recognized by their peers and celebrated by all.

Recommendations for practice

My five-year plan is the basis for my recommendations for practice. The plan has eighteen points, designed to develop the individual in the context of the school environment and promote teacher leadership and shared governance. The points are not sequential, nor are they to be considered a step-by-step process. Many items are developed, practiced, reviewed, and revised continually, and some are operational procedures. Teachers and administrators follow the same process. The basic requirements of our practice include using action research, surveying school personnel, considering alternatives, reviewing policy and law, reaching consensus, and publishing results. The nature of the task determines the involvement of the administration. For example, it is necessary to have administrative input on a committee with the charge of changing the master schedule, but it is not necessary on a committee charged with developing a new course.

Formal structures

Formal structures help establish stability within schools. These are the positions that are traditionally viewed as teacher leadership roles. Some positions are appointed, while others are elected by colleagues.

• A leadership team was created to solicit broad-based input from the faculty and to broaden the base of decision making at the school. The department chairpersons, media specialist, and administrators were included as part of the leadership team. The leadership team meets once per week (utilizing released time) and discusses and makes decisions on any and all items brought to the table. Minutes are recorded and published by a school secretary. It is important that the administration respond to questions and concerns with a nondefensive posture. Petty or minor items are addressed as soon as possible. The posture of the administration is supportive and facilitating rather than controlling. When the group makes a decision, everyone must support the decision, including (especially) the principal.

• A staff development committee was organized to make decisions concerning the distribution of staff development funds for the local school. The committee consists of four faculty members, two of whom are on the systemwide committee. The members are all teacher volunteers, and all serve for a period of two years. It is the committee's responsibility to solicit input from the faculty, to develop goals for the school year, and to make judgments on the allocation of funds, based on those goals. Currently our goals include technology education and teaching methods for at-risk students. All local staff development funds are controlled by this committee, and the school administration has no control or veto power.

• A volunteer teacher leads the process of school accreditation and compliance with state standards. A teacher leader in our school has responsibility for maintaining records, making time lines, answering questions, and leading the faculty steering committee. Our school is accredited by the Southern Association of Colleges and Schools (SACS) and the Georgia Accrediting Commission. After our SACS ten-year site visit in 1994, our school decided, under teacher leadership, to move to a school renewal process. The process was teacher-driven.

• The textbook adoption committee, which also serves as a curriculum development committee, was established. The central office provides leadership through the curriculum office to coordinate the K–12 efforts. I believe that the implementation phase of textbook adoption and curriculum development needs particular support from the school administration. Departmental reviews, peer observations, and student and parent surveys are essential elements of a successful implementation. Collection, interpretation, and dissemination of data is totally managed by teacher leaders.

• The budget process is in the process of being reorganized to include teacher and departmental decisions concerning schoolwide and individual allocations. I will be moving our budgeting procedures from a focus on prior-year expenditures to a focus on instruction and student needs. Teacher leaders have already changed schoolwide patterns of paper and copying use in order to reallocate dollars to other instructional materials.

• Teacher recognition and participation in celebrations is an integral part of our school. All teachers and administrators march with students in the graduation ceremony each year. We do this as a means of celebrating our success and to show our pride in our students. The "teacher of the year" shares the honor of presenting diplomas with the superintendent of schools.

• School publications such as student and teacher handbooks and curriculum guides include a directory of teachers and administrators, listing their degrees and the institutions of higher learning where they earned them. This helps to identify teachers and their individual achievements and enhance professional pride.

• The hiring of new staff has become a task that involves faculty as equal members of the interview and selection team. The typical configuration of a team hiring a teacher or administrator includes two teachers, one of which is a department chairperson, and an administrator. The team screens applications, interviews candidates, and makes recommendations for selection. To date all team recommendations have been supported by the superintendent and the board of education.

Informal structures

Informal structures are more difficult to monitor and maintain, but in my opinion they have a greater influence on teacher leadership. I have included in this list several of the informal means I use to develop teacher leaders. The list is by no means complete, and the majority of new ideas come from the faculty and staff as they begin to use action research to influence how they go about teaching and learning.

- I keep track of leadership opportunities provided or taken advantage of by faculty, staff, and administration members. I record events, projects, special recognition ceremonies, staff development, grants, teacher training, workshops, conferences, and miscellaneous items. I do this as a means of inclusion rather than exclusion, because I believe it is important for each teacher to be given the opportunity to lead or to take part in a leadership activity.

- Staff development is often a vehicle for teacher leadership. Teachers who attend staff development workshops are asked to share their experiences with their colleagues by publishing their learning and insights. We have an internal newsletter that provides the vehicle for teachers to publish throughout the school.

- A level of trust must be developed within the staff to truly create an environment where teachers feel they are respected as leaders. I believe that in order to exhibit the belief that teachers are colleagues, you must allow them the same level of control and influence that you have as an administrator. As I interact with teachers I am always honest (even when it hurts), consistent, and straightforward. Any teacher will be reluctant to take on a leadership role without being comfortable with the level of trust received from the school administration. To this end I submit an evaluation form on the principal to the entire staff at the conclusion of each school year. I do so with a self-created instrument that allows for a rating scale as well as written responses. During preplanning the next school year, I use the evaluation as a means of structuring discussion concerning my operation of the school. As a team we also evaluate all faculty activities, including meetings, preplanning and postplanning, staff development, and work days. These evaluations are used by the leadership team to restructure the activities in the following year.

- A series of nonacademic activities were developed to encourage teacher involvement with students. These events, such as a spring musical and a winter concert, give teachers an opportunity to work with students and community members outside the classroom. Teachers exhibit leadership by their involvement and are viewed by students and community members in a different context. We have had strong participation in these activities from students, faculty, administration, central office staff, and community members.

• I not only recognize a "teacher of the year" in a formal cere- mony, I continue to showcase the teacher informally throughout the year. I choose the final faculty meeting of the year to recognize the next teacher of the year and provide him or her with a gift bear- ing the school crest and the individual's name. Teachers of the year are identified throughout the year at public functions such as par- ent events, homecoming, awards ceremonies, and graduation. I provide release time and join them when they attend luncheons and ceremonies honoring teachers and students. This recognition in our school has become part of the tradition.

• Like many schools, we provide staff development in the sum- mer, for a variety of reasons. The staff development committee will approve some teacher requests, the central office will approve some requests, and other teachers will go on their own for additional schooling or individual improvement. I invite two teachers to attend a different conference each year. I select teachers from the list who have not yet demonstrated leadership but whom I feel will contribute to the school as leaders in some capacity in the future. They are selected from different departments and attend the same conference. I select a conference with a nationally known speaker and a topic of interest to our school. I fund it totally through the principal's fund and require nothing in return. I do provide the teachers with the opportunity to share with others and to publish if they choose. I have found that these teachers are more enthusi- astic and optimistic when they return to school. Each of the teach- ers has chosen to take on an active leadership role following these staff development activities.

• We have developed a partnership with a major corporation and university. As part of the partnership agreement, the corpora- tion provides our staff with technical training. We invite teachers to self-select for this training, provided they are willing to return to the school and train the members of their department. Each training session provides another opportunity for teachers to be leaders. These teachers then become a resource for others as an expert in the area of training. I always take part in one of the local training sessions in order to demonstrate to teachers that administrators are learners along with them.

• It is important for principals to take the time to engage in professional dialogue with all teachers and to become learners in those relationships. Teacher observation and evaluation often become routine, consisting of a short time in the classroom and a brief written evaluation. State law and board of education policy may require an evaluation; however, the principal can and should also make the process a minor part of the dialogue between the administration and teachers. I spend time with teachers, asking them nondirective questions about students, the curriculum, and their teaching techniques. Teachers appreciate the opportunity to share what they are doing and to discuss their professional concerns. Teacher leadership is enhanced as a result of nonthreatening, face-to-face conversation between the principal and teachers.

• When the principal or administrators attend a workshop or conference, a teacher is always invited to attend. It is important that all teachers have the opportunity to attend a workshop from time to time. I believe that if a workshop is important for administrators, it is also important for teachers.

• As our school grows and changes, we are being recognized by other schools and systems as a leader in the areas of governance and teacher leadership. When I am asked to speak or present a workshop for a school or conference, I always invite a teacher to present along with me. This helps demonstrate teacher leadership and focuses the success on the teacher.

Conclusion

Our school is a long way from achieving our goals, and our teachers are a long way from becoming the leaders that I envision, but we are light years ahead of where we were two years ago. Our goals are in range, I believe, because our teachers are beginning to view themselves and their students as part of the solution rather than part of the problem. Leadership is emerging consistently and deliberately from unexpected sources.

Critics may argue that a school with so many leaders really has no leadership, resulting in inefficiency and a lack of organization. Teachers have always been team players who understand group dynamics. To be a leader on one project and a follower on another is second nature to teachers. I believe that the administrator who learns to follow and support others in their attempts to lead will ultimately have a better-organized, more-powerful school. I don't believe that learning and leadership are necessarily efficient, tight processes, however, and therefore I don't apologize for being part of a school that is not efficient. I endorse a continual process of growth and change.

Our teachers have demonstrated that they are ready for systemic change revolving around schoolwide instructional issues. I believe this is a direct result of their ability to govern the environment in which they work, the level of trust they experience in the administration, and the continual emergence of teacher leadership within the school.

We continue to grapple with more efficient ways to use the time we have. The faculty has committed more personal time to school issues, and our plans for the future include the use of staff retreats and a new schedule for the high school.

Our culture changes have come as a result of teacher leadership. There is little animosity about changes because they come as result of teacher-initiated and teacher-supported projects. An essential part of our growing culture is the incorporation of change and reform as a key ingredient in our collaborative vision. I articulate the shared vision as often as possible in my speech and my actions, and I encourage others to lead the way.

References

Barth, R. S. *Improving Schools from Within: Teachers, Parents, and Principals Can Make the Difference.* San Francisco: Jossey-Bass, 1990.

Darling-Hammond, L. "Reframing the School Reform Agenda." *Phi Delta Kappan*, 1993, *74*, 753–761.

Glickman, C. D. *Renewing America's Schools: A Guide for School-Based Action.* San Francisco: Jossey-Bass, 1993.

Odden, E. R., and Wohlstetter, P. "Making School-Based Management Work." *Educational Leadership*, 1995, *52*, 32–36.

Schlechty, P. C. "Leading Cultural Change: The CMS Case." In A. Lieberman (ed.), *Building Professional Culture in Schools.* New York: Teachers College Press, 1988.

Schlechty, P. C. *Schools For the 21st Century: Leadership Imperatives for Educational Reform.* San Francisco: Jossey-Bass, 1990.

Sergiovanni, T. J., and Starratt, R. *Supervision: Human Perspectives.* New York: McGraw-Hill, 1988.

Starratt, R. J. *Leaders with Vision: The Quest for School Renewal.* Thousand Oaks, Calif.: Corwin Press, 1995.

JAMES R. KAHRS *is currently principal of Oconee County High School in Watkinsville, Georgia. He was recognized as one of eight educational pioneers in the state of Georgia in the 1995 publication* Democratic Principals in Action, *by Blase, Blase, Anderson, and Dungan, published by Corwin Press.*

Two teacher leaders assert that true leadership enables practicing teachers to lead reform efforts and alter the hierarchical nature of schools. In this chapter they point to the professional development school as an answer to barriers to leadership. These barriers include the nature of teachers, the structure of schools, teachers' egalitarian ethic, and their lack of decision-making power. Reflecting on the nine-year-old Learning-Teaching Collaborative, the authors identify five areas of leadership development. To institutionalize teacher leadership, the authors suggest reforming the workplace, redefining the role of the principal, and supporting the role of teacher as leader.

3

Teacher leaders and power: Achieving school reform from the classroom

Katherine Boles, Vivian Troen

TEACHING IS NOT a profession that values or encourages leadership within its ranks. Our public schools are based on a nineteenth-century industrial model of management, with a hierarchical organizational structure and an adversarial relationship between management (the administration) and labor (teachers) (Tyack, 1974). Like factory workers of the 1800s, teachers in the 1990s all have equal status. Leadership opportunities are extremely limited.

Recognizing the serious flaws in this traditional model, school reform reports of the late 1980s made compelling recommendations for teachers to provide active leadership in restructuring the

NEW DIRECTIONS FOR SCHOOL LEADERSHIP, NO. 1, FALL 1996 © JOSSEY-BASS PUBLISHERS

nation's schools. The reports acknowledged the centrality of class-room teaching and emphasized the importance of creating new roles for teachers—roles that extend teachers' decision-making power into schoolwide leadership activities.

The report of the Carnegie Forum on Education and the Econ-omy (1986) went so far as to say that without teacher support "any reforms will be short lived" and that the key to successful reform "lies in creating a new profession . . . of well-educated teachers pre-pared to assume new powers and responsibilities to redesign schools for the future" (p. 2).

Teacher leadership has emerged as a new buzzword in the educa-tion community's search for a quick fix for school ills. It is tempt-ing to ignore the fact that teacher leadership roles—generally in curriculum, school improvement, and professional development—are often limited in scope and vision and subject to easy cancella-tion when budgets are cut.

School districts proudly point to examples of teacher leadership, no matter how minimal their impact on day-to-day operations. That's somewhat like calling a banana republic a democracy if a few of its citizens are allowed to vote—the bulk of the populace is resentful of those who do vote, and the supreme power at the top of the administrative ladder is watchful and suspicious lest the idea of participation spread and disrupt the status quo.

We suggest that true teacher leadership enables practicing teach-ers to reform their work and provides a means for altering the hier-archical nature of schools. What is needed is a school culture in which classroom teachers are fully empowered partners in shaping policy, creating curriculum, managing budgets, improving practice, and bringing added value to the goal of improving education for children. Why has it been so difficult to create and sustain leader-ship roles for teachers?

The nature of teachers

Concerned with teaching practice and primarily focused on life in the classroom, teachers have been reluctant to think of themselves as leaders outside the classroom (McLaughlin and Yee, 1988). They often view with discomfort the idea of assuming quasi-administrative or expanded teaching functions. Experience has taught them that teacher leadership and risk taking are not valued in their school. As Barth (1991) so aptly stated, "A teacher is like a mushroom. It thrives in the darkness, but when it sticks its neck out, its head immediately gets cut off."

The structure of schools

Leadership in schools has traditionally consisted of top-down mandates, with little input from classroom practitioners (Tyack, 1974). Developing programs and reforms has never been considered the work of teachers. Instead, it has been the teacher's job to carry out plans developed by others at higher levels in the school hierarchy (Lortie, 1975). Overlaying this organizational architecture has been the issue of gender. Since the mid nineteenth century, teaching has been accepted as woman's work, or as Catherine Beecher (a leader in a movement to spread education across the country) called it, "woman's true profession" (quoted in Hoffman, 1981, p. 36). Women's traditional role was to follow, not lead. Tyack referred to the newly feminized schools of the nineteenth century as "pedagogical harem[s]," where many women taught and a few men directed (1974, p. 45). Such "programmatic and behavioral regularities" (Sarason, 1971, p. 62) continue to this day in our schools, and they make it seem as inappropriate for a teacher to assume leadership as it would seem for an assembly line worker to suggest how to improve the assembly line.

The egalitarian ethic

The issue of the equality of all teachers inevitably arises in any discussion of teacher leadership. Teachers in Johnson's study of 115 "very good" teachers (1990) remarked that they and their colleagues often do not take advantage of available opportunities to exert formal influence because of the "norms of equity that [discourage] individual teachers from stepping forth and taking the lead, and skepticism about the prospects for success" (p. 1). Other researchers have noted that the "equal status" norm is so strong that, though principals may acknowledge the existence of team leaders, teachers may deny that they exist (Cohen, 1981) or doubt their effectiveness (Arikado, 1976). And in their study of the cultures of teaching, Feiman-Nemser and Floden describe a "norm of non-interference" that prevents teachers from using their regular interactions at staff meetings, in lunchrooms, and at the photocopy machine "to discuss their work or to collaborate on shared problems" (Feiman-Nemser and Floden, 1986, p. 509). The disinclination of teachers to discuss educational practice, to follow the lead of their peers, and to recognize the efforts of their peers who take leadership roles must be factored into any discussion of teacher leadership.

Teacher leadership introduces status differences based on knowledge, skill, and initiative into a profession that has no provision for them (Little, 1988). Seeing some teachers get attention and respect by doing something new and different only intensifies feelings of powerlessness in other teachers and prompts them to defend their turf. This brings up what is probably the most important obstacle of all to the institutionalization of teacher leadership: the issue of power.

Lack of decision-making power

Often left undiscussed in the dialogue surrounding "shared decision making," "school-based management," and "the professionalization of teaching" is the issue of power. Decision-making power in schools is carefully allocated. Decisions about classroom policy—what to teach, how to use time, and how to assess progress—are made by teachers (Johnson, 1990). But other decisions that affect teachers' work—scheduling, class placement, assignment of specialists, and the allocation of budget and materials—are made at higher levels of the school bureaucracy. This norm, by which teachers feel (and often are) powerless to affect schoolwide policy, is broadly accepted by teachers and administrators alike. The prevalent view of power as a "zero-sum game," in which a gain in one area requires a loss in another, makes it difficult for teacher leaders to emerge in schools. Principals who fear they will be relegated to roles as operational managers if teachers assume leadership roles actively oppose such changes (Koppich, 1993).

College-school collaborations: The professional development school movement

Though leadership by teachers is increasingly seen as a key to reforming schools and improving the teaching career, it is extremely difficult for this new form of leadership to emerge in schools as they currently exist. Given this reality, the professional development school (PDS) looms large in the minds of those who wish to foster school reform through teacher leadership. PDSs focus on improving the education of children, enhancing the professional development of pre-service and in-service teachers, and altering the relationship between colleges and schools (Levine, 1992). More than two hundred PDSs now exist, in various stages of development (Darling-Hammond, Bullmaster, and Cobb, 1995).

Teachers are affected in various ways by a PDS experience. In a PDS, teachers' roles are expanded and their responsibilities increased. PDSs recognize the unique perspective of the classroom practitioner and provide a forum for teachers to voice their knowledge of the teaching craft, a knowledge that "often challenges the more formal knowledge base that university professors represent" (Miller and Silvernail, 1994). Furthermore, teachers in a PDS are expected to exert influence beyond their classrooms and to play important roles in the larger arena of the school, school district, and professional community (Levine, 1992; Darling-Hammond, 1994). This makes PDSs fertile ground for the emergence of teacher leaders.

The Learning/Teaching Collaborative

In 1987, together with Wheelock College faculty member Karen Worth, we created the Learning/Teaching Collaborative (LTC), a partnership between the Boston and Brookline, Massachusetts, public schools and Wheelock and Simmons Colleges. The goal of the collaborative was to provide opportunities for teachers to assume new professional roles while remaining in the classroom. Administered by teachers, the LTC is now in its ninth year. It has grown from one team of three classroom teachers and a half-time special education teacher in one school to nine teams of four to ten teachers in six public elementary schools. Even in an era of diminishing resources, the LTC has demonstrated steady growth.

Four components provide the framework for the LTC:

1. *Team teaching.* Teachers, functioning as a team, share curriculum and children. Five hours per month are allocated for team meetings outside the school day. In addition, principals have arranged common planning time for teachers so that teachers, their interns, and the college supervisor can meet on a regular basis.

2. *School-university collaboration.* Graduate student interns from Wheelock College or Simmons College work full-time in the teams during the entire school year. A teacher and college faculty member teach the Wheelock interns' graduate-level curriculum seminar together. Other teachers present guest lectures on their particular areas of expertise, and a number of classroom teachers teach courses in reading and math methods at the two colleges. A steering committee composed of college and school faculty representatives and administrators from each of the participating institutions governs the LTC and meets four times per year. Subcommittees meet throughout the year to handle budgeting, recruitment of interns, the professional development of teachers, parent involvement, and public relations.

3. *Special education and bilingual inclusion.* In a number of the teams both special needs and bilingual children are fully main-

streamed. Special education and ESL teachers are members of the teams; they consult with teachers and give some direct service to children.

4. *Alternative professional teaching time.* Each classroom teacher is provided with a minimum of one day a week (six hours) away from teaching duties to assume an alternative role—curriculum writer, researcher, student teacher supervisor or college teacher. This "alternative-professional teaching time" (APT time) is facilitated by the full-time presence of teaching interns.

Developing a new paradigm for teacher leadership

In our studies of the LTC over its nine-year history (Boles, 1991; Boles and Troen, 1994), we have discovered that PDSs have had a profound effect on teachers' willingness to assume leadership roles. The forms of leadership assumed by teachers at PDSs are quite different, though, from traditional models of teacher leadership, and this difference has forced us to rethink our evolving definition of teacher leadership.

In the past, teacher leaders were chosen to assist beginning teachers, to fulfill roles in supervision, to develop curricula, or to serve in part-time administrative positions (Lieberman, Saxl, and Miles, 1988). Such teacher leaders were carefully screened and selected; they often worked alone and frequently found their teacher colleagues resistant to their leadership.

In the LTC, a form of leadership has developed that is assumed by many individuals. In this paradigm, teachers continue to be professionally independent. The powerful norm of professional equality is not violated. Teachers develop expertise according to their individual interests. The role of teacher leader has been reconfigured to make it available to more teachers.

Our findings have confirmed studies indicating that teachers care less about moving into a few administratively designated leadership positions and more about enlarging their professional roles and enhancing the professional aspects of their careers (McLaughlin and Yee, 1988). Our paradigm of teacher leadership does not introduce career ladders or set up a limited number of roles that can be accomplished by only a very few individuals. It creates an interactive community of teachers collaborating for improvement and experimentation in their schools.

Though this description of leadership differs from the traditional model, it does contain most of the acknowledged components of legitimate leadership. In this new paradigm, teacher leaders satisfy the following criteria:

1. *Leaders are role models who facilitate the development of those around them.* Teachers in the LTC provide powerful role models for interns, colleagues, and the children they teach. They work as researchers, curriculum writers, mentors, and members of governing committees, directly influencing all the members of the collaborative.

2. *Leaders challenge the status quo.* When LTC teachers leave their classrooms one day a week to assume expanded roles, they challenge the norm of the "good teacher," whose job is defined as giving direct services to children full-time. Teachers who regularly coteach, discuss their practice, and visit one another's classrooms are risk takers who challenge the status quo of teaching as an isolated act conducted in the privacy of the individual classroom.

3. *Leaders have influence in domains outside the classroom.* As a result of their work in the collaborative, LTC teachers conduct research and publish their results in professional journals. Others have assumed roles in research organizations beyond the school or have developed college coursework or redefined the role of the college supervisor. These roles have expanded the teachers' domains of understanding and decision making and have enabled them to behave more knowledgeably and confidently in the school arena.

It would appear that the LTC provides a model for a new culture in these teachers' schools. And it has done this without removing talented teachers from the classroom. We do not present the LTC as the "ultimate answer" to teacher leadership; rather, we offer it as one model for implementing a new leadership paradigm. Once we move beyond paradigms that reinforce the current hierarchical nature of schools, new possibilities become available. It is even possible to respect the norm of teacher equality and develop ever-more-powerful forms of teacher leadership.

Facilitating forces for teacher leadership

Three aspects of the LTC have been central to the development of these new forms of teacher leadership:

Team teaching and collaboration. The team became a forum in which teachers could experiment with their teaching and expand their knowledge base. The LTC gave the teachers a common frame of reference and a common language and collegial support to make pedagogical innovations. Team teaching eliminates teacher isolation. LTC teachers talk about their teaching and feel energized by team discussions. They trust their colleagues, feel accountable to other team members for the work they do, and receive the collective latitude needed to take professional risks.

Use of time. Most reform efforts do not adjust the school day to give teachers more time to accomplish their work and assume new roles. By providing full-time graduate student interns to work in teachers' classrooms, the LTC has managed to fulfill the promise of creating more time for teachers. Not only are there two teachers in the classroom during most of the week, but the presence of the interns through APT time gives teachers six hours a week away from the classroom to pursue their own professional development.

All the LTC teachers have used APT time to assume new responsibilities. They speak about how busy they are, but they do not complain about an inability to accomplish their work because of a lack of time. Nor do they describe feeling guilty about being away from their children or being unable to accomplish their primary role of classroom teacher.

Leverage beyond the classroom. The college connection enables LTC teachers to expand their professional influence and gain leverage outside their schools without leaving classroom teaching. In addition, working in the collaborative has given the teachers more power than they had as individual classroom practitioners. Since it was understood that the teachers were part of a specific program with set guidelines and roles, the teachers found it easier to request

APT time and common planning time from their principals. Principals, recognizing that APT time invigorated their veteran teachers, were willing to oblige.

Obstacles to teacher leadership

The forms of leadership described in this chapter developed over a long period of time, and the course of change has been slow and uneven. Every aspect of the collaborative has been fraught with difficulties, and the teachers have often felt that every forward step was accompanied by a step backward. Even when teachers believed philosophically in the changes they were implementing, the culture and norms of their school and of the teaching profession contradicted what they were doing and slowed or halted their progress.

Accustomed to autonomy, teachers were frustrated by the LTC's team structure, which constricts their independence. They had been used to changing their original lesson plans when their students seemed to be going in a different direction. Now that was impossible, since the team schedule mandated that they teach certain subjects at certain times.

Efforts to include special needs children in mainstream classrooms confronted the special needs bureaucracy, and teachers were forced to stand their ground and pull strings to ensure that their model remained intact. Teachers found themselves at odds with people higher up the school ladder, and they worried that they would alienate powerful individuals. And, indeed, they did.

Team meetings took valuable time from the school day that would have been used to call parents, photocopy materials, prepare lessons, and so on, and teachers balked. They found themselves coming late to meetings or canceling them altogether when demands on their time became overwhelming.

The time that had been carefully carved out for APT time was not easy to use. At first teachers had no idea how to manage this unscheduled time. Work in classrooms was the work they knew, and entering the uncharted territory of teacher research or curriculum development was daunting. In addition, the classroom was the teachers' power base, the domain in which they had most control, and teachers found that they did not take the time that had been allocated to them. Thus teachers moved ahead in fits and starts, sometimes wondering why they were involved in this project. The process was developmental, though, and over the nine-year history of this PDS it is possible to trace a slow change in the teachers' attitudes and behaviors. Too often, the success of change projects is measured after only a year or two, and the projects are found to come up short of their goals. What is evident from the LTC's experience is that change is possible, teachers can model the way for change, change does not come easily, and change takes much longer than anticipated.

Ultimately, there has been significant change in many aspects of teachers' professional lives as a result of this PDS. This has been due in large part to the perseverance of the teachers involved. We do not want to minimize the effort it took to make the changes described, but the purpose of this chapter is to demonstrate that such changes are possible and that teachers can assume new forms of leadership that have not yet been imagined in schools.

Areas of leadership development

LTC teachers have experienced leadership development in the following five areas:

- Pedagogical innovation
- Pre-service teacher education
- Curriculum development
- Research
- Governance

Pedagogical innovation

The teachers changed their instructional practices as a result of working in teams. Most of the teachers now coteach with other team members, special education teachers, and interns. In addition, special education teachers consult weekly with mainstream teachers to implement modifications for special needs children. Cross-graded work in reading and science occurs in a number of teams, cooperative learning marks the classrooms of many of the teachers, and interdisciplinary teaching has become the norm in many classrooms.

Teachers speak of the amount of "ongoing dialogue" they have with one another. One remarked that since joining the collaborative, she has become a much better teacher "because of the dialogue, because of sharing ideas, because of feedback from other people, because of chances for exposure to other ways of doing things." Directly related to the teachers' work in teams is an increased sense of responsibility and accountability. The teachers are responsible to one another and for all the team's children. With this new feeling of responsibility comes a new experience of collegial accountability; the teachers remark that they feel accountable to one another in new ways. As one teacher stated: "If you are the only person in the class, you organize and run your program as a one-person operation. When you work on a team, you count on the contributions of all the members. It's a real change in the way I plan and how I work. I'm much more accountable to other people now. I used to be able to close the classroom door and do what I wanted."

The experiences of the teachers we have interviewed reinforce Little's findings (1987) that teachers working in teams exert high levels of "reciprocal influence" (p. 13) on one another. Because their teaching has become more public, and perhaps because it is no longer a secret, private act (Fullan, 1992), these teachers now venture beyond the classroom.

Pre-service teacher education

The LTC and other PDSs significantly alter teachers' role in pre-service education, enabling them to assume new leadership roles with interns and at the college level. The teachers at the LTC have more control over their interns' experiences than they ever had over student teachers, and they are beginning to influence the structure of pre-service education.

Pre-service teacher education provides the linchpin for the PDS, increasing teachers' authority and influence in a new realm—the college. The teachers, in collaboration with college faculty, supervise the interns and write the interns' evaluations and recommendations. Comparing their current experience with previous experiences with student teachers, the classroom teachers say they feel more accountable for the interns. They attribute this feeling to the amount of time the interns spend in the team and to the classroom teachers' increased responsibility for the interns' education. Teachers report having a greater stake in what happens to their interns; they note that the time factor is a crucial part of their increased interest in the interns' future. As one interviewee commented, "You are accountable to your intern to provide [a] quality education so they see what good education is. You are accountable to your intern to present progressive teaching, not standard, basic, boring, traditional teaching—'whip out a book and teach.' You are accountable to show the standards of what you expect your intern to live up to. You are accountable. You are doing a service to the college, and the college is doing a service to you. You are accountable to them. There is a whole lot that is affected by this program if you screw up."

Curriculum development

The teachers routinely develop new curricula at their grade levels and assume leadership in districtwide curriculum revision. Teachers see the importance of improving their curriculum: the structure of the PDS factors time for curriculum development into the school day. Principals arrange for teachers to have common planning time at least once a week, and paid after-school or weekend meetings for curriculum development are a regular part of each team's work. An added impetus for curriculum development occurs as new curriculum ideas are introduced to the teams by college supervisors and interns, who share theories and knowledge at team meetings and in informal conversations with the mentor teachers.

A number of teachers use their six hours per week away from classroom teaching to develop new curricula. Over the years a number of the LTC teachers have been involved in math curriculum development during their APT time through Technical Education Research Centers, Inc., a research organization located in Cambridge, Massachusetts. The school districts adopted this new math curriculum largely as a result of these teachers' recommendation, and now these teachers are involved in supporting the implementation by direct instruction, modeling, and peer coaching.

Teachers are developing curriculum collaboratively with the resources of the college and the assistance of the interns and their peers. They have the time they need during the day to experiment and develop the curriculum. As one teacher stated, "We are trying to reimagine curriculum and trying to establish a role of reconfiguring the way kids learn. I would say that those are the two main roles as a member of the team."

Research

Teachers in the LTC have assumed leadership in classroom-based action research. Over the course of the collaborative's history, the use of APT time to conduct classroom-based research has become increasingly appealing to the teachers. At least one teacher in each team has assumed the role of teacher-researcher, and one team has decided that each of its members will conduct some form of research during the school year and that this research will be supported through a research seminar facilitated by a faculty member from Wheelock College.

One teacher-researcher noted that research has been a "tremendously beneficial activity," that as a result of conducting research he has become "much more reflective about my role in the classroom." His research on children's writing choices and their attitudes about writing have led him to a reexamination of his own teaching and an effort to improve his teaching of writing through "listen[ing] carefully to the voices of writers as they [participate] in the process of writing fiction." Teachers see the effect of their research on the children they teach. According to one teacher, "You can see the by-products of your research, the halo effect . . . the kids feel empowered and feel important, so the benefits are there."

Teachers have become interested in going beyond the role of "teacher as deliverer of knowledge." Instead they want to *create* knowledge, by working on research in their classrooms, across schools, and in communities. They have come to believe that teachers have a responsibility for systematic research and inquiry directed at improving their practice.

Governance

All LTC teachers have gained leadership experience governing the collaborative. Though the organizational structure of the LTC has changed over its nine-year history, a consistent aspect has been that every teacher must play an active role in its governance. Teachers understand that this teacher-initiated, teacher-managed collaborative depends on each of them for its continuation, and every teacher serves on one of the collaborative's five governing committees. This work has taught them administrative skills as well as how to build teams and reach a consensus. It has introduced them to fund-raising and to the complicated work of managing the collaborative's budget. In addition, it has introduced them to the politics of school change and given them an awareness of the fragility of this teacher-initiated PDS.

Teacher leadership and power

An interesting parallel can be drawn between PDS facilitating forces and the "power tools" described by Kanter (1977) in her work on organizational change in the corporate world. Kanter's power tools—"information (data, technical knowledge, political intelligence, expertise); resources (funds, materials, space, time); and support (endorsement, backing, approval, legitimacy)"

(p. 158)—enable individuals to understand their organization and make important changes in it. The LTC has provided teachers with many of these tools, which few teachers can marshal on their own. The teachers acquire information through teaming, teacher research, and collaboration with the college. The collaborative's primary resource is time; other resources include access to budgets and to materials purchased with grants. Support is provided through the relationship with the college, the cohort of teachers, and increasing recognition and institutionalization of the LTC by both the school system and the college.

In addition to acquiring new power tools, the teachers in LTC have assumed many of the same attributes as the "entrepreneurial innovators" described by Kanter. The teachers "make connections, both intellectual and organizational. . . . They reach beyond the limits of their own jobs-as-given. . . . They are good builders and users of teams" (p. 212). And, like their corporate counterparts, "they are aided in their quest for innovation by an iterative environment, in which ideas flow freely, resources are attainable rather than locked in budgetary boxes, and support and teamwork across areas are the norm" (p. 162).

Making connections

Teacher leaders from the LTC have made significant connections and sustained contacts with individuals inside and outside their institution. They have left the isolation of the classroom behind, gaining new information about the functioning and culture of their school. They are able to maneuver (tentatively at first, but more and more confidently) in the larger realm. Connections mean that they have new roles. As one classroom teacher stated, "I'm a mentor teacher to an intern. I'm the team leader. The college liaison and I became involved in the responsive classroom. Last year and this year I've given seminars to the interns about the responsive classroom. . . . I was intimidated, but I loved it. I'm going to do the same thing with another instructor and her interns this year." Another teacher commented on his participation in a national PDS forum: "I have broader contacts and perspectives. It's given me a new understanding of the university and what role it has to play in teacher training. What we're working toward [in] teacher education should be more intertwined with the school. We should be thinking along the way doctors and lawyers train. The give and take between teachers and students in student teaching should be increased." Interns and teachers speak about the importance of the school-college connection in helping them be on the "cutting edge." The connection has empowered them; it makes them more likely to take risks, and it opens new professional opportunities.

Reaching beyond predefined limits

Respondents valued the opportunities the PDS provided for them to broaden their roles and increase their influence, both in their own institution and in the partner institution. A teacher remarked, "I can have input on how things happen. I don't throw up my hands because I can't effect changes. I have a common goal of teacher training with the college. . . . Teaching at the college level has caused me to be more self-conscious about why I do what I do and [whether] it's a good way to do it." When college courses are taught at the school site, teachers and administrators recognize that it is a powerful statement from the college of its respect for the school. It makes the PDS a more visible entity and helps the school community appreciate its investment in the school site.

My role in the collaborative goes beyond being a cooperating teacher. I am more involved in the curriculum at Wheelock than I ever was before, because now I teach a course there. In all cases, teachers, interns, and college faculty feel that their status is enhanced and their influence expanded as a result of having moved beyond their traditional roles. The combination of new perspectives and increased information allow them to operate in new domains.

Becoming good builders and users of teams

There is a common understanding of the importance of the team. Teachers remark that the team gives them an incentive to try new ways of doing things and that team teaching broadens their view of the curriculum. One teacher remarked, "I like everything about teaming. I like thinking about ideas, working with colleagues. I have to say it's been very stimulating for me. I come to school energized." Some individuals use the team as a support, as a base for action. College faculty use it as an entree into the schools. Being part of the collaborative team gives teachers leverage with their principals when schedules are being determined.

PDSs create an iterative environment in which ideas flow freely, resources are attainable, and support and teamwork are the norm. One teacher's description of what he learned reflects Kanter's description of the importance of cross-pollination in simultaneous renewal: "I've learned a great deal through my relationships with interns and the college and have improved my practice, which is now embedded in theory and current research. I teach a course on numeracy and literacy at the college, which continues to be informed by my experimentation in the classroom. I share with my team what I've learned by teaching the course at the college." Some participants comment that the LTC's steering committee gives more people access to resources at both institutions, and teachers get support from that group for their individual efforts at both sites. The collaborative's structure connects people, keeps the paths of communication open, and maintains the flow of information. One teacher noted, "This work has affected my understanding of the school and college, because I've gotten to know college people on a personal level. I realize that they're not different. I can see how things work at the college."

Teacher leadership and educational reform

What we've learned about teacher leadership has ramifications for the entire educational reform movement. Teacher leadership must be institutionalized in many different settings in order to have an impact on schools throughout the country. In conclusion, we offer three suggestions that will further the goal of institutionalizing teacher leadership.

1. *Reform the workplace.* Working in isolated classrooms and competing for scarce resources, teachers often eye one another suspiciously as they lead their children down the school corridors. The "egg crate" mold of the school, with its secretive and competitive aspects, must be broken. When a philosophy stressing collaboration and risk taking replaces teacher isolation, teacher leadership will emerge. When teachers work in teams and teaching becomes a more public act, teachers will venture beyond the classroom. Teams can become a testing ground in which teachers can take risks with their teaching and expand their knowledge base.

The egalitarian ethic must be reconsidered, not rejected. Currently, teachers are not at all equal. They live in competitive isolation, competing for the scarce resources available to them, knowing that some teachers have more access to these resources than others. If teaching were truly egalitarian, we would value each teacher's contribution to the education of children, at the same time recognizing individual areas of expertise and celebrating leadership initiatives.

Teachers need time for reflection and opportunities to conduct professional inquiry. What we are calling for cannot be accomplished at the end of a long day in the classroom. Time in the work day must be restructured so that it can become a resource, not one more reason why teachers are unable to assume leadership.

2. *Redefine the role of the principal.* The principal must become a collaborative leader of continuous improvement in the school as an organization. The larger goal of the principal must be to transform the culture of the school to allow collaborative groups of teachers to organize learning. Principals can exercise instructional leadership by shaping the organization, climate, and resources of the school. They must be actively involved in developing teachers' commitment to exerting leadership. Leithwood and Jantzi (1990) found that successful principals use six broad strategies:

- Strengthen the school's culture (to promote teacher leadership).
- Stimulate and reinforce cultural change through a variety of bureaucratic mechanisms.

- Foster staff development.
- Engage in direct and frequent communication about cultural norms, values, and belief.
- Share power and responsibility with others.
- Express cultural values through the use of symbols.

Preparation programs for teachers and principals must be restructured so that all understand the importance of developing a community of leaders within schools. Principals must be provided strategies to facilitate teachers' taking on leadership roles, and they must participate in teaching teachers how to be leaders.

In sum, the role of the principal, with its plethora of burdensome administrative tasks, must be redesigned so that principals have the time to become educational leaders in their own right.

3. *Support the role of the teacher as leader.* The term *teacher leader* will remain no more than an oxymoron if the education community continues to treat it as such. Teachers themselves must advocate for the creation of leadership roles. Building on their expertise in teaching and learning and their understanding of the needs of children, teachers must now acquire leadership skills and an understanding of organizational theory and behavior in order to facilitate change.

Teachers must become resources for one another, and they must become accountable to one another for the work they do. No longer should teachers stand by helplessly as teacher colleagues "sink or swim" in their first few years in the classroom. No longer can teachers turn a blind eye to the teacher who is behaving unprofessionally or to those who are just not working hard enough.

School districts must evaluate principals on their ability to foster teacher leadership in their buildings, and they must provide incentives and rewards for teachers who take the lead in tackling tasks and solving problems. Teacher unions must cultivate leadership among their members and take responsibility for educating teachers in the political and organizational aspects of their work. Colleges of education must recognize the importance of teacher leadership and strengthen their commitment to teaching those skills as a required component of teacher education.

If we are to change the professional environment of our schools, we must develop external connections. We must foster better relationships between school professionals and parents, colleges, state departments of education, federal agencies, and the business community.

Our own experience in the LTC demonstrates that empowered teachers can create successful models to change today's schools. Myriad difficulties and obstacles confront the institutionalization of teacher leadership, but we must continue this struggle if we are to carry school reform from the nineteenth century into the twenty-first.

References

Arikado, M. S. "Status Congruence as It Relates to Team Teacher Satisfaction." *Journal of Educational Administration*, 1976, *14*(1), 70–78.

Barth, R. S. Speech delivered at Professional Development Forum, sponsored by the Commonwealth of Massachusetts and the Field Center for Teaching and Learning, May 15, 1991.

Boles, K. C. *School Restructuring by Teachers: A Study of the Teaching Project at the Edward Devotion School.* Doctoral dissertation, Harvard University, Cambridge, Mass., 1991.

Boles, K. C., and Troen, V. "Teacher Leadership in a Professional Development School." Paper presented at the annual meeting of the American Educational Research Association, New Orleans, 1994.

Carnegie Forum on Education and the Economy. *A Nation Prepared: Teachers for the Twenty-First Century.* New York: Carnegie Forum on Education and the Economy, 1986.

Cohen, E. "Sociology Looks at Team Teaching." *Research in Sociology of Education and Socialization*, 1981, *2*, 163–193.

Darling-Hammond, L. (ed). *Professional Development Schools: Schools for Developing a Profession.* New York: Teachers College Press, 1994.

Darling-Hammond, L., Bullmaster, M. L., and Cobb, V. L. "Rethinking Teacher Leadership Through Professional Development Schools." *The Elementary School Journal*, 1995, *96*(1), 87–106.

Feiman-Nemser, S., and Floden, R. E. "The Cultures of Teaching." In M.C. Wittrock (ed.), *Handbook of Research on Teaching.* New York: Macmillan, 1986.

Fullan, M. "Arming Yourself with Knowledge of the Change Process." Speech given at the annual meeting of the American Educational Research Association, San Francisco, 1992.

Hoffman, N. *Woman's "True" Profession: Voices from the History of Teaching*. Old Westbury, N.Y.: Feminist Press, 1981.

Johnson, S. M. *Teachers at Work*. New York: Basic Books, 1990.

Kanter, R. M. *Men and Women of the Corporation*. New York: Basic Books, 1977.

Koppich, J. E. "Rochester: The Rocky Road to Reform." In C. T. Kerchner and J. E. Koppich (eds.), *A Union of Professionals: Labor Relations and Educational Reform*. New York: Teachers College Press, 1993.

Leithwood, K., and Jantzi, D. "Transformational Leadership: How Principals Can Help Reform School Culture." Paper presented at the annual meeting of the American Educational Research Association, Boston, 1990.

Levine, M. *Professional Practice Schools: Linking Teacher Education and School Reform*. New York: Teachers College Press, 1992.

Lieberman, A., Saxl, E. R., and Miles, M. B. "Teacher Leadership: Ideology and Practice." In A. Lieberman (ed.), *Building a Professional Culture in Schools*. New York: Teachers College Press, 1988.

Little, J. W. "Teachers as Colleagues." In V. Richardson-Koehler (ed.), *Educators' Handbook: A Research Perspective*. New York: Longman, 1987.

Little, J. W. "Assessing the Prospects for Teacher Leadership." In A. Lieberman (ed.), *Building a Professional Culture in Schools*. New York: Teachers College Press, 1988.

Lortie, D. *Schoolteacher*. Chicago: University of Chicago Press, 1975.

McLaughlin, M. W., and Yee, S. M. "School as a Place to Have a Career." In A. Lieberman (ed.), *Building a Professional Culture in Schools*. New York: Teachers College Press, 1988.

Miller, L., and Silvernail, D. "Wells Junior High School: Evolution of a Professional Development School." In L. Darling-Hammond (ed.), *Professional Development Schools*. New York: Teachers College Press, 1994.

Sarason, S. B. *The Culture of the School and the Problem of Change*. Boston: Allyn & Bacon, 1971.

Tyack, D. B. *The One Best System—A History of American Urban Education*. Cambridge, Mass.: Harvard University Press, 1974.

KATHERINE BOLES *is lecturer in education at Harvard Graduate School of Education, Cambridge, Massachusetts.*

VIVIAN TROEN *is a teacher leader at the Edward Devotion School, Brookline, Massachusetts.*

*This author presents a unique perspective on involving teachers
meaningfully at the district level. She stresses the importance of
a comprehensive approach that includes systematic identification and selection of potential teacher leaders, a wide range of
teacher leadership roles and opportunities, and the necessary
development and support. The essential characteristics and
skills needed by teacher leaders are synthesized from the literature. Specific roles for teacher leaders in school system district
offices are described. The author concludes that teacher leadership is not only a tool for school site reform but also a tool for
districtwide renewal.*

4

Moving beyond the school: Teacher leaders in the district office

Joellen P. Killion

TEACHERS BECOME INVOLVED, share their learned wisdom, and
influence others at their own school. Similar opportunities outside
one's school are more elusive, but more and more teachers are seeking ways to influence the larger education system and to be heard
and recognized beyond their own classroom and school.

Efforts to involve teachers meaningfully at the district level have
fallen short of providing teachers with genuine opportunities to
become leaders. School districts will benefit from the untapped
potential and promise of teacher leadership if they establish a comprehensive program that includes systematic identification and selection of potential teacher leaders, a range of districtwide opportunities

NEW DIRECTIONS FOR SCHOOL LEADERSHIP, NO. 1, FALL 1996 © JOSSEY-BASS PUBLISHERS

to engage teachers in leadership roles, and the necessary development and support for teacher leaders.

As school districts strive to redesign the educational system to meet the growing demands of the public and the increased challenges students bring into the classroom, the leadership and influence of teacher leaders is even more critical. Sergiovanni (1995) asserts that traditional models of leadership imported from business and industry fall short of the type of leadership required in schools and school districts. For school districts, teacher leaders can serve as critical bridges between traditional and emerging leadership models.

Studies of teacher leadership report that teachers serve in a wide variety of capacities. Smylie and Denny (1990) found that teacher leaders support their colleagues and help them fulfill their traditional classroom responsibilities and improve their practice. They also found that, not surprisingly, teacher leaders' activities are often restricted by the time demands of their traditional teaching roles. Role limitations that keep teachers from exerting their leadership capabilities at the school level are even more confounding for teachers who wish to extend their influence beyond the school site.

This chapter outlines considerations for central office personnel who wish to establish a teacher leadership program to maximize the benefits of leadership to their district and teachers. The chapter reviews strategies for identifying and selecting teacher leaders and characteristics that contribute to the success of teacher leaders. In addition, there are recommendations for preparing and supporting teacher leaders through professional development to further extend and refine their skills. Lastly, the chapter includes examples of techniques for meaningful district-level roles for teacher leaders.

My work as a district staff developer has afforded me many opportunities to identify teacher leaders, to provide professional development experiences to further challenge teacher leaders, and to work with teacher leaders in many other diverse ways. Of particular interest to my work with teacher leaders is the search for appropriate methods to promote continued personal and professional development for more experienced teachers. Tapping the expertise of teachers and encouraging them to assume leadership roles is one way to promote experienced teachers' professional development and increase human resources within a district.

Systematic involvement of teacher leaders

Encouraging teacher leadership is intentional; it does not occur by chance. To reap the greatest benefit for both the teacher and the school district, central office personnel and teachers need to work together to design a comprehensive teacher leadership program that fosters equitable access to leadership roles, allows the district to discover the potential of untapped leadership candidates, and values the contribution of teacher leaders. Districts must commit to select, engage, develop, and recognize teachers who serve in leadership roles.

Identifying and selecting teacher leaders

Identifying and selecting teacher leaders are best done systematically rather than voluntarily. Voluntary selection may result in teachers who are enthusiastic and willing but lack the necessary skills to be successful. Not surprisingly, willingness and enthusiasm have not been cited in the literature as significant characteristics leading to success as a teacher leader. Although they are certainly necessary for success, these characteristics alone are not sufficient to meet the challenge of leading one's peers. Systematic selection affords districts the opportunity to identify teachers who have honed some of the skills necessary for district-level leadership and who want to further refine their personal and professional skills. Several processes exist for identifying and selecting teacher leaders.

Application

Teachers might apply for various leadership roles as they would for other positions. Experience with this process suggests that the application process broadens the opportunity to serve to include all interested teachers. The application process may indicate that the role of teacher leader is more substantial than that of volunteer. Further, this selection process permits an alignment of applicants' expertise with the identified role and responsibilities. When one district sought teachers to serve as district conflict mediators, for example, a notice outlining the responsibilities and desired skills was sent to all teachers. Interested teachers who felt they met the criteria for the role submitted an application outlining how they met the identified criteria. In an application process, the submitted applications were carefully reviewed by a broad-based team of stakeholders. Interviews were then held and the best candidates selected.

Nomination

Another technique for identifying teacher leaders is a nomination process. Administrators or other teachers are asked to identify teachers to assume leadership roles, or teachers can be invited to nominate themselves. When another district developed its mentoring program, principals were asked to nominate several candidates from their school to participate in the training. Principals were given a description of the program and a list of the desired mentor qualifications, for use in making their nominations. Since principals know their staff—their teaching ability and their interpersonal skills—better than central office personnel, they are better able to recommend possible mentors. The nomination process permits principals and others who know which teachers are ready for a challenge or have the necessary expertise for a particular project to recommend those individuals for leadership roles. Principals and others are also able to identify teachers who have the potential for leadership but need encouragement to seek a leadership opportunity.

Invitation

Another way to identify and select teacher leaders is to issue a specific invitation. Sometimes as projects arise and particular expertise is needed, teachers are invited to serve as leaders. For example, a recent curriculum revision project in one district required the perspective of a classroom teacher to ensure that the curriculum was "user-friendly." A teacher with expertise in the content area and with strengths in group facilitation was invited by the director of curriculum to lead a small group of teachers revising the curriculum document. Personal invitation allows central office personnel to tap teachers with specialized knowledge and skills for a particular project or responsibility. Invitation can also draw out teachers who may not be aware of the leadership opportunities available to them.

Teachers invited, nominated, or selected through an application process have increased credibility and esteem as recognized leaders. These methods of identifying teacher leaders suggest, through their formality and their alignment with districtwide leadership behaviors and beliefs, that teacher leadership is a respected and valued asset in the school system.

Characteristics of teacher leaders

Teachers who provide leadership in district-level initiatives are "instructional leaders"; their influence extends well beyond the more traditional school-based leadership roles of department, grade-level, or committee chairperson. Pellicer and Anderson (1995) define instructional leadership "as the initiation and implementation of planned change . . . that results in substantial and sustained improvement in student learning. . . . The exercise of instructional leadership calls for providing vision and direction, resources and support to both teachers and students" (p. 16).

To provide instructional leadership, teacher leaders must have the necessary knowledge, skills, and attitudes. A number of research studies have identified essential characteristics of teacher leaders. According to Lieberman, Saxl, and Miles (1988), for example, teacher leaders must

- Build trust and rapport
- Examine issues within an organizational context
- Build skill and confidence in others
- Use resources wisely and efficiently
- Deal with change
- Engage in collaborative work

O'Connor and Boles (1992) point out the following characteristics of teacher leaders:

- Understanding of politics, power, and authority
- Skill in managing interpersonal relationships
- Communication skills
- Understanding of group dynamics
- Presentation skills
- Organizational skills
- Ability to change

Hatfield, Blackman, Claypool, and Master (1987) stress teacher leaders' flexibility, patience, technical competence, and ability to engender respect. Teacher leaders do need all of these attributes and skills to serve in leadership roles. The complexity of their tasks and the scope of their responsibilities determine which characteristics teacher leaders need to be most successful in their roles. Two attributes of particular importance for district-level teacher leaders merit further discussion. Teacher leaders who develop a systemwide perspective and operate from a value of stewardship have the best opportunity for success.

Systemwide perspective

Since teachers have traditionally worked solo as masters of their own classroom, their understanding of the intricate relationships among the various components of the entire school district may be limited. Teacher leaders often need time and opportunities to develop an understanding of systems thinking and to apply that understanding in their work at the district level. Teacher leaders learn on the job to appreciate how closely connected all the different aspects of their school district are and to be able to anticipate the effects of their work throughout the school system. Lieberman, Saxl, and Miles (1988), in their study of teacher leaders, report that teacher leaders enter their new roles with a sensitivity to individuals; however, they also need to acquire an appreciation for teachers, principals, and the school community as a whole. Teacher leaders "found that what had worked in more narrowly defined positions would not work in the pursuit of a larger, common vision" (p. 150).

Stewardship

Pellicer and his colleagues (1990) state that instructional leadership begins with an attitude from which values and behaviors emerge. Stewardship is an essential attribute for teacher leaders. Block (1993), in his book *Stewardship*, defines stewardship as "the willingness to be accountable for the well-being of the organization by operating in service, rather than in control, of those around us. Stated simply, it is accountability without control or compliance" (p. xx). Teacher leaders must accept accountability without control, service over self-interest, and trust over dependency. Committing to these values and behaviors challenges even the most experienced leaders. Teachers who attempt to serve as leaders but lack an orientation toward stewardship quickly lose credibility, effectiveness, and the ability to influence others. Teachers who have a wide array of skills, broad knowledge, a healthy attitude about service to others, and enthusiasm and willingness to serve will have the greatest success as leaders.

Preparing and supporting teacher leaders

Teacher leaders benefit from ongoing professional development to further refine and develop their leadership knowledge and skills. Providing a systematic program aimed at developing teacher leaders, including training, coaching, support, and reflection, is a key responsibility of school district personnel who work with teacher leaders. Opportunities for practice in a team situation or in partnership with a cofacilitator or coleader, feedback and support from a mentor, and involvement in a variety of leadership activities are strategies for job-embedded staff development for teacher leaders.

Pellicer and Anderson (1995) conclude that while many teachers are willing to assume instructional leadership roles, "they lack the necessary preparation in the knowledge, skills, and attitudes required to function as instructional leaders within loosely coupled school organizations" (pp. 20–21). Teacher leaders need many diverse skills and expertise in areas that are not typically included in teacher preparation programs. Thus school districts need to offer a professional development program specifically for teacher leaders.

A program for the continuous development of teacher leaders should consist of several components. The first is assessment. Some teachers who seek leadership opportunities at the district level have already had experiences with leadership at their schools, and their skills vary significantly. Before prescribing a program of professional development, it is best to conduct some assessment of teachers' past experiences, strengths, and areas for development. With a mentor or coach, a teacher leader might explore what knowledge, skills, and attitudes he or she wishes to develop and which areas must be developed, given his or her current responsibilities. The second component of a systematic professional development program for teacher leaders is a plan for developing or identifying personal and professional goals, indicators of success, strategies for achieving goals, time lines, resources needed, and ongoing assessment strategies. Training through a wide range of methods is the third component. Opportunities to read extensively, apply skills, receive frequent feedback and coaching, and team with an experienced leader are other essential components. Since learning often occurs from practice rather than from formal training, reflection on one's work is another critical component in the development of teacher leaders. A comprehensive professional development program for teacher leaders might also include formal evaluations of the outcomes resulting from the teacher leaders' work. The results could illustrate the vital nature of the work of teacher leaders.

The more common skills for which teacher leaders need training and development are outlined below. This is by no means a comprehensive list of the skills teacher leaders need to refine, but these are the skills that lend themselves most easily to a training program. Other skill areas such as timing, assessing organizational culture, and understanding politics and power are best acquired on the job through practice, coaching, and reflection.

Group process and development

In most cases teacher leaders' roles require them to work closely with other educators and very often in team situations. Teacher leaders are successful teachers first, and successful teachers often concentrate heavily on their classrooms and so become isolated from other adults. The realities of working collaboratively with others, especially in large groups with varied participants, require dramatically different skills. It is helpful for teacher leaders to understand group development and to have a repertoire of strategies for helping groups structure their work and techniques for building teams.

Interaction and communication skills

The act of leading others or bringing about change requires effective communication, including written, oral, and nonverbal communication. As Book (1995) says, "Competent communicators have . . . a repertoire of communication strategies from which to draw and the ability to use criteria to select the appropriate strategies given the audience and context, to implement the strategies effectively, and finally to evaluate the success or failure of the communication attempt and to remedy the communication as needed" (p. 150). Effective leaders need communication to inform, persuade,

express feelings, exchange ideas, and create meaning. Most classroom teachers are effective communicators; however, the signifi-
cance of their communications when they are in leadership roles
requires careful attention to their communication decisions. Most
teacher leaders benefit from ongoing learning and practice in effective communication.

Facilitation

Helping groups achieve an outcome is an essential task of teacher
leaders. Teachers, who have for so long been directors of their own
classrooms, often must struggle with facilitating the efforts of others. Facilitation skills involve knowing how to help a group take
primary responsibility for solving its problems and mitigate factors that hinder the group's ability to be effective. Facilitation
involves technical knowledge and skills that extend well beyond
the preparation of classroom teachers—knowledge and skills that
are only developed through years of practice, coaching, and reflection.

Understanding change

As Pellicer and Anderson (1995) explain, "Leadership involves
change, and change requires the ability to take others where they
would not normally go" (p. 17). Teacher leaders must promote and
support change in others. Most teacher leaders are comfortable
with change. They embrace with excitement opportunities to
improve their own practice. Their eagerness to promote continuous improvement of the educational system is often the driving
force behind their seeking leadership roles. Yet, not all stakeholders
within the educational community are comfortable with or embrace
change. Many struggle to maintain the status quo. Teacher leaders
need to understand change theory and processes and the effects of
change on individuals and systems. They need to develop a range
of interventions for assisting people and their organization with
change. Training can help teacher leaders understand change and
develop skills for assisting others.

Conflict resolution

Change inevitably brings conflict. Teacher leaders who not only understand the factors that lead to conflict but also have a range of strategies for managing and resolving it will be more successful. It is particularly important for teacher leaders to understand that conflict is a natural part of change and to develop a healthy perspective about conflict. Strategies for resolving interpersonal and group conflict will be particularly useful to teacher leaders. As with other leadership skills, teachers have not been adequately trained in conflict resolution techniques.

Designing and delivering learning experiences

As Gardner (1989) says, "Leaders teach. . . . Teaching and leading are distinguishable occupations, but every great leader is clearly teaching" (p. 18). Many teachers assume leadership roles that give them the opportunity to teach others in staff development programs. Yet, teaching students, which most teacher leaders have done for years and at which they excel, differs from teaching adults. Many teachers will say that other teachers are their worst students. The reasons for this are not difficult to determine. Teachers are busy people who have extremely high standards and expectations for their own learning experiences. They want information tailored to their classrooms, delivered in ways that not only ensure that they learn but also model new strategies they might use in their classrooms. Techniques for designing and delivering training and other types of professional development experiences, working with adult learners, and supporting the transfer of new learning to the workplace are fundamental skills for teacher leaders.

Problem analysis

Leaders do not solve problems alone. They often guide others to solve their problems. Effective teacher leaders, rather than solving problems for others, use strategies to help them solve their problems themselves. Problem analysis skills involve identifying the various dimensions of a problem, examining the contexts or conditions leading to the problem, and analyzing the probable causes of the problem. Once the problem has been thoroughly analyzed, teacher leaders guide others in the problem-solving tasks of establishing criteria for evaluating solutions, generating solutions, testing their feasibility, and choosing the best solution. In addition to knowing the necessary steps for analyzing and solving a problem, the teacher leader benefits from having strategies for guiding groups through the problem-analysis and solution-formulation processes.

Decision-making skills

In today's school districts, shared decision making abounds. Efforts to meaningfully engage all stakeholders in the decision-making process have increased as school districts encourage involvement of the entire school community. It is not uncommon for decision-making groups to include students, teachers, administrators, parents, business and industry leaders, and nonparent taxpayers. Even the decision-making processes have changed. Today, consensus has replaced simple majority vote as the preferred decision-making methodology in groups. Knowing various decision-making methods, selecting the most appropriate method for a particular situation, and having a repertoire of strategies for helping others reach a decision with the chosen method are critical skills for teacher leaders.

The potential of teacher leadership is too significant to leave undeveloped. Too often districts move teachers into leadership roles without the necessary professional development to ensure their success. Realizing the promise of teacher leadership requires careful attention to the continuous professional development of teachers' leadership knowledge, skills, and attitudes.

Teacher leadership opportunities at the district level

Many opportunities exist at the district level for teachers who wish to assume a leadership position and influence change. Districts' procedures for selecting, preparing, and rewarding teacher leaders is a major roadblock in making these opportunities available, however. Districts hesitate to ask teachers to take on additional responsibilities when their day-to-day classroom responsibilities are so demanding. Teachers are hesitant to take on additional responsibilities for a variety of reasons. Lieberman (1988) cites the egalitarian ethic, which views all teachers as equal regardless of their experience or ability, as one obstacle to teacher leadership. The tension that exists between teacher unions and school district administrations often discourages teachers from engaging in roles beyond the classroom. Despite these obstacles, one midsized school district (twenty-three thousand students) offers a variety of rewarding and challenging opportunities for teacher leaders. This district, Adams Twelve Five-Star Schools, Northglenn, Colorado, is described below.

Staff development

Teacher leaders make up the largest percentage of the pool of district trainers. Many teachers eagerly accept the opportunity to share their expertise with other teachers by becoming trainers in districtwide or site-specific staff development programs. These teachers bring the realities of the classroom and the gifts of their experience and wisdom to the training program. All teachers are offered the opportunity to participate in a preliminary train-the-trainers program, and if they wish they may continue with the program and become a staff development trainer. Trainers participate in a twenty-four-hour course on training strategies, receive coaching and support from experienced trainers, and are evaluated annually. Trainers are compensated at an hourly rate for their work, and they must demonstrate competence to become a district-approved trainer. Most teacher leaders provide courses for other teachers in curriculum and instruction, while others offer training on leadership skills.

Florence Jensen was known to the teachers in her building as an expert on learning centers. When the district's curriculum was revised, teachers throughout the district asked for help in learning more about designing and managing learning centers that would promote more active learning and higher engagement among students. The director of staff development knew just who could help. She invited Florence to design and teach a staff development course to help teachers construct and manage learning centers aligned with the new curriculum. Florence's class was such a success that it was repeated several times.

Curriculum coaches

Curriculum coaches are experienced, well-trained teachers who have release time to support teachers as they implement new district curriculum. Teacher leaders work with teachers in a particular subject area within their school and in neighboring schools. They may coplan, coteach, demonstrate, observe, offer feedback, problem solve, and coach teachers. Curriculum coaches receive training in the content area curriculum and instructional strategies as well as in coaching skills. Curriculum coaches are selected by their principal and recommended to the director of curriculum. They receive no supplemental compensation for their work. They are respected by their peers as master teachers and receive public acknowledgment and personal gratification for their willingness to help others.

Colleagues of Margaret Washington often sought her advice on teaching the new math curriculum. They knew that as a result of her work with the National Council of Teachers of Mathematics, Margaret was an expert in the new math standards. When Margaret's district realized that many teachers would benefit from the support of teachers like her, it initiated a cadre of classroom teachers to provide in-class support in the implementation of the district's new language arts and math curriculum. Margaret applied for the role of a curriculum coach. One day a week she visited teachers in three elementary schools. She helped them plan lessons, demonstrated new instructional strategies, observed them using new techniques, provided feedback, helped them locate needed resources, and taught classes on the new math content. Margaret was excited to share what she knew about math with teachers who felt less comfortable in that content area. In the process, Margaret added to her own repertoire of skills and strategies to improve her own classroom teaching.

Curriculum developers

Teacher leaders who serve as curriculum developers have an in-depth knowledge about a particular curriculum area and have some understanding of curriculum design. They are usually invited to serve as curriculum developers by personnel in the district's curriculum and instruction department. Teachers who serve as leaders in the area of curriculum development often have opportunities to participate in training programs to extend their knowledge in the curricular area. Typically their work is done after the school day and in the summer, with some limited compensation or with salary advancement credit. In some situations teachers have been fully or partially released from their classroom responsibilities for a semester or two to oversee a particular curriculum development project.

Gary Garcia and Jenny Stewart had just finished an advanced degree in reading. Both were brimming with recent research and wanted to share what they had learned. When the director of curriculum was forming a committee of teachers to review and recommend revisions to the district's reading curriculum, she naturally called Gary and Jenny. They volunteered to serve on the committee with eight other teachers during the remainder of the school year and prepare recommendations for the director. They both found a receptive audience in their fellow committee members, who were eager to learn what Gary and Jenny had discovered from their recent research.

Task facilitators

Task facilitators make a group's task easier to accomplish by providing structure and processes for completing the task. As more and more small task forces have been formed for problem solving and decision making, the district has realized a tremendous need for facilitators who can work with these groups and assist them with their work. Initially, a specially selected group of teachers meeting the established criteria were invited to participate in a training program to become facilitators. After their training, they were invited to serve as facilitators for various district task forces or project teams. Their training consisted of a twenty-hour class in facilitation skills, and some have volunteered to participate in advanced training. In most cases, these facilitators volunteer their services; however, if the project extends over ten hours, they are compensated at an hourly rate. The facilitators meet periodically in a support group to share their experiences and continue their own development. Shortly after the initial group received their training, an increased demand for facilitators necessitated providing more facilitators. The training program is now available to all employees to develop their leadership potential.

David Brown recently completed the district's staff development course in facilitation skills. He enjoyed the change of pace from his regular teaching responsibilities and looked forward to facilitating a team soon. A colleague of David's in another school knew David was eager to apply his newly learned skills, so she recommended David to her principal as a possible facilitator for the task force on multi-age classrooms. The principal believed it would be in the best interest of everyone if a neutral individual from outside the school facilitated this task force, so he called David. David gladly accepted the opportunity to learn and apply his new skills for the duration of this three-month project.

Mediators

Mediators help groups and individuals in the district resolve conflicts. Teachers were invited to apply to become mediators. The announcement listed criteria for the role and a description of mediators' responsibilities. Applications were reviewed by a team of people. Successful candidates participated in a twenty-hour training course on mediation, conducted practice mediations, received feedback on their performance, and were assigned to co-mediate situations as they arose in the school district. Mediators receive no compensation for their work unless the situation requires a considerable amount of time. Most mediators report that the intrinsic reward of helping people resolve their problems is sufficient compensation for their time.

Vicki Greenleaf applied to become a member of the district's mediator cadre. She wanted a challenge and knew that if she were successful, she would not only learn some valuable skills she could apply in her high school classroom, she would also help people throughout the school district resolve their differences in a healthy and productive manner. After she successfully completed the training, Vicki mediated several disputes. She helped two parents reach a constructive resolution in a disagreement about one student's behavior. She helped three third-grade teachers at one school air some differences and reach an agreement about how to work together in a more collaborative fashion. Vicki was learning and helping others at the same time. She felt renewed.

Mentors

Mentors work closely with novice teachers to acculturate them into the school system and assist them in becoming successful teachers. New state educator licensure regulations required a formal induction program for all provisionally licensed teachers in the district. The induction program requires novice teachers to work collaboratively with a mentor. Many district teachers have been nominated by their principals and been selected through an application process to be district mentors. District mentors are teachers with proven expertise in instructional strategies, curriculum, and classroom management who are willing to support and coach a novice teacher. They work with new teachers both inside and outside their own school. They receive training in mentoring skills and are assigned to work with a new teacher for at least one year. They also work with experienced teachers who need additional support in their classroom from peer support teachers. Mentors receive some release time for working in new teachers' classrooms, and a stipend. They participate in monthly support groups with other mentors to continue their development, sharing their experiences and analyzing case studies.

Bob Bartlett, a twenty-five-year veteran teacher, was five years away from retirement. He had heard about the district's new mentoring program and remembered with fondness the teacher who had helped him make it through his first years of teaching. He wondered if he might be able to provide the same type of support to a new teacher. After some consideration, Bob applied to become a mentor and was pleased to learn that he had been accepted. Bob participated in the training program and was assigned two brand new teachers to mentor. He enjoyed guiding, supporting, coaching, and encouraging these teachers. He discovered that someone finally appreciated his years of wisdom and expertise and even wanted to hear his war stories. Bob was eager to talk about teaching, students, content, and the contributions teachers make to society. He mentioned to his wife one night that he felt he could teach for another thirty years if it continued to be this much fun.

District innovation facilitators

When districts undertake new initiatives, additional human resources are often needed to initiate, implement, and institutionalize the change. In their study of innovations, Hord, Rutherford, Huling-Austin, and Hall (1987) confirmed the importance of the principal as the key to change in schools. They also found that others play significant roles in promoting change, however. These people are often school and central office–based personnel such as teachers, curriculum coordinators, and assistant principals, who balance and extend the principal's leadership and support. Teachers are frequently hired to assume this form of leadership, to assist others in the necessary role and behavior changes required to implement innovations. Teacher leaders who are respected by their peers and administrators, have years of successful experience with students, understand the demands on teachers' time, and are committed to the vision of the innovation are hired to provide additional support for those involved. In these situations, the district innovators serve as second, third, and fourth change facilitators who have specialized expertise and are easily accessible to those responsible for implementing the change. Some examples of district innovation facilitators include teachers who serve as members of the district's technology cadre and diversity training cadre and those who are support group coordinators for teachers implementing a new reading program. These teacher leaders build the capacity of other teachers to become leaders. District innovation facilitators may receive some limited compensation or salary advancement credit for their extra duties, or if the project demands additional personnel, they are fully or partially released from their classroom for the duration of the project.

Denise Romero always wanted to be a teacher. As a student in high school, she wondered why there were so few Hispanic teachers as role models for students. She vowed then that she would help other Hispanics receive a good education and make a positive contribution to their community. When the district announced its desire to help teachers learn more about the needs of minority students, Denise volunteered to help. She served as a member of the Diversity Cadre, a group of staff members from throughout the district who developed a comprehensive plan to forward the district's diversity initiative. Eventually Denise became a trainer in the district's diversity courses, served as the chair of the Hispanic Education Committee, coached teachers in integrating multiculturalism into their curriculum, and worked with student groups at the middle school and high school. Denise's contributions to the district were recognized formally when she was named Hispanic Educator of the Year by a local business consortium.

Clinical professors

Through a partnership arrangement with several local universities, master district teachers are released partially or fully from their classroom responsibilities for two years to work in collaboration with the university pre-service and intern programs. These teacher leaders teach undergraduate education classes and coordinate the required pre-service educational experiences. Clinical professors also teach district staff development courses on working effectively with pre-service teachers and supervising student teachers. They teach a course in classroom management skills to student teachers within the district. By far, their most rewarding opportunities are coaching intern teachers and serving as clinical faculty at the university, where they are highly respected by university faculty as teaching experts. Clinical professors are selected through a competitive application process and must demonstrate expertise in coaching on a performance task during the interviewing process. They receive no additional compensation for their work. They do benefit, however, from numerous opportunities to participate in a wide range of professional development experiences during their tenure as clinical professors. In their annual evaluations of their experience, clinical professors report that this leadership opportunity affords them tremendous personal and professional growth.

Phil Rothman's desire was to teach teachers someday. He often thought of earning a doctorate so he could teach at a college or university. He was a master teacher and was recognized by his peers as someone who was creative, sensitive, in touch with current research in education, and eager to try new things. When the annual vacancy notice came out for the district's clinical professorship, Phil decided that he would apply. The position would afford him the opportunity to teach undergraduate classes at the nearby university, supervise student teachers, and mentor new teachers. Phil knew he would be great in this role, and he was eager to learn what it was like working with less experienced teachers. He was delighted to learn that he had received the position. As school started in the fall, Phil's job changed dramatically. He prepared a syllabus for his college course in elementary math methods, met with three student teachers and their cooperating teachers to outline expectations for the semester, and counseled two new teachers to whom he had been assigned. As he was helping one of his new teachers put up her first bulletin board at eight o'clock the night before the first day of school, Phil remarked that his fourth-grade classroom, which he had left last spring, seemed like a breeze compared to the multifaceted job he would have for the next several years. Yet, he would not trade the opportunity to learn and grow for anything. He was determined to make the most of the next few years.

Conclusion

As Pellicer and Anderson (1995) assert, "Without question, teachers are the best and most abundant source of leadership available to schools. Teacher leaders remain the last best hope for significantly improving American education. If teachers fail to embrace their responsibility to provide the leadership needed in our schools, then all educators fail. And if administrative bureaucrats do not provide the conditions and support necessary for teacher leadership to flourish, then all educators fail. In the final analysis, the efforts of teacher leaders at the forefront of change will be only as successful as the bureaucracy allows them to be" (p. 21).

Teacher leadership is a powerful tool for districtwide educational renewal. It demands that school districts establish comprehensive programs to identify and select aspiring teacher leaders, develop their capacity, and find meaningful opportunities to engage them in challenging roles with significant responsibilities. Numerous factors are converging to realize the tremendous potential of teacher leaders. Declining human resources, increased numbers of experienced teachers who seek new challenges and meaningful ways to influence others throughout their entire school system, and the importance of teachers' perspective on reform efforts offer districts a window of opportunity to realize the potential of teacher leadership.

References

Block, P. *Stewardship*. San Francisco: Berrett-Koehler, 1993.

Book, C. L. "Communicating Leadership and Change." In M. J. O'Hair and S. J. O'Dell (eds.), *Educating Teachers for Leadership and Change: Teacher Education Yearbook III*. Thousand Oaks, Calif.: Corwin Press, 1995.

Gardner, J. W. *On Leadership*. New York: Free Press, 1989.

Hatfield, R. C., Blackman, C., Claypool, C., and Master, F. *Extended Professional Roles of Teacher Leaders in the Public Schools*. Unpublished manuscript, Michigan State University, East Lansing, 1987.

Hord, S. M., Rutherford, W. L., Huling-Austin, L., and Hall, G. E. *Taking Charge of Change*. Alexandria, Va.: Association for Supervision and Curriculum Development, 1987.

Lieberman, A. "Expanding the Leadership Team." *Educational Leadership*, 1988, *45*(5), 4–8.

Lieberman, A., Saxl, E. R., and Miles, M. "Teacher Leadership: Ideology and Practice." In A. Lieberman (ed.), *Building a Professional Culture in Schools*. New York: Teachers College Press, 1988.

O'Connor, K., and Boles, K. "Assessing the Needs of Teacher Leaders in Massachusetts." Paper presented at the annual meeting of the American Educational Research Association, San Francisco, April 1992.

Pellicer, L. O., and Anderson, L. *A Handbook for Teacher Leaders*. Thousand Oaks, Calif.: Corwin Press, 1995.

Pellicer, L. O., and others. *High School Leaders and Their Schools*. Volume II: *Profiles of Effectiveness*. Reston, Va.: National Association of Secondary School Principals, 1990.

Sergiovanni, T. J. *Leadership in the Schoolhouse: How Is it Different? Why Is it Important?* San Francisco: Jossey-Bass, 1995.

Smylie, M., and Denny, J. "Teacher Leadership: Tensions and Ambiguities in Organizational Perspective." *Educational Administration Quarterly*, 1990, *26*(3), 235–259.

JOELLEN P. KILLION *is staff development specialist in the Adams Twelve Five-Star Schools in Northglenn, Colorado. She is also former president of the National Staff Development Council.*

A state's commitment to the professional development of teacher leaders is described by two trainers. A professional development model consisting of personal assessment, changing schools, influencing strategies, and planning for action is described. Program evaluation data shared by the authors are descriptive of the skills acquired, leadership roles taken, and impact of the actions of teacher leaders. The authors describe how the state's efforts have resulted in emergent teacher leadership, but not without problems. Their conclusion suggests that learning by teacher leaders is more powerful than legislation in accomplishing school reform.

5

Developing teacher leaders: A state initiative

Pamela Hart, Bruce Baptist

WITH THE REALIZATION that teachers can create, carry out, and evaluate educational reform efforts, region- and state-level administrators in Florida committed resources, beginning in 1991, to support the development of teachers as leaders. Launching professional development for teachers to prepare for leadership roles was a state priority. The state implemented a training program, Leadership Development for Teachers (LDT), to teach leadership skills to teachers who do not want an administrative position but still want to influence teaching and learning in their school. We work with teachers throughout the state, assisting them in their efforts to take active leadership roles.

NEW DIRECTIONS FOR SCHOOL LEADERSHIP, NO. 1, FALL 1996 © JOSSEY-BASS PUBLISHERS

Based on our state's experience over the past five years, this chapter focuses on the context for teacher leadership, the professional development model used, and the evaluation of the impact of teacher leadership on our teachers, their students, and our schools.

Context for teacher leadership

In 1991 the Florida state legislature passed a significant school reform bill, known as Blueprint 2000. The intent of this law was to loosen institutional constraints and to challenge each school to meet the needs of its students. School councils or school improvement teams now provide a forum for teacher leadership in every school. Teachers are involved in changing the curriculum, designing new programs, and challenging the status quo. Blueprint 2000 has given teachers and other stakeholders the responsibility and flexibility they need to design effective programs, free from prescriptive state mandates.

Response to a perceived need

To meet the mandate to improve the state's schools, five regional educational networks offer comprehensive leadership development services to schools. These networks facilitate the sharing of information and resources across school district and university boundaries, fostering collaboration among districts on issues of mutual concern. The regional networks focus attention on the development of leadership skills that address the process of leading change in an educational environment.

The belief that empowering teachers to use new leadership knowledge and skills in their personal and professional lives is directly related to the success of school improvement led to the development of a five-day course, "Leadership Development for Teachers" (LDT). The regional networks provided this program in conjunction with other professional development experiences designed to help schools work through the change processes demanded by the state, school districts, and communities.

Program assumptions

The LDT program is a professional development experience that offers teachers an opportunity to develop strategies for accomplishing their work with school improvement. The following assumptions led to creation of the program:

- Teachers, even those who are already leaders, do not see themselves as leaders.
- Moving from formal leadership to shared leadership in schools is consistent with school reform.
- Involving teachers in decision-making processes taps the talent, competencies, and enthusiasm of teachers and helps maintain their internal motivation for teaching.
- A critical mass of teacher leaders, empowered with new knowledge and skills, can change schools.
- Changing the principal at a school will be less disruptive if teachers are empowered to continue the change effort.

Program approach

Teachers volunteer to attend the LDT program with the intent of improving their leadership skills in order to assist in solving problems at their school. The program addresses the needs of these teachers, who desire to broaden their focus beyond the classroom but not as a prerequisite for an administration position. Individual teachers, teams from schools, or an entire "feeder pattern" of school teams attend the training. We have seen the best results when teams of teachers are involved, because the teams help support their individual members when they return to their schools. At times, assistant principals or parents join the teams of teachers so they can help the teacher leaders back at their school.

The LDT model

Four major components make up the program: personal assessment, changing schools, influencing strategies, and planning for action. Teachers write in journals to reflect on their experiences, then share their concerns with "journal partners," discussing the implications of what they are learning for their school. Teachers are asked to apply their learning in portfolio assignments related to their home school setting. Working with a "home" team throughout the program enables teachers to get to know a smaller group, allowing them to more easily give and receive feedback.

Personal assessment

Until teachers examine their own beliefs, it is difficult to understand what influences their colleagues' behavior. The personal assessment component of the program invites teachers to engage in a series of self-assessment activities. This type of activity encourages teachers to examine their own beliefs and why others may or may not share those same beliefs. First, the teachers assess themselves in regard to selected characteristics of teacher leaders. Looking at well-documented characteristics of teacher leaders helps participants realize they may already be assuming leadership roles.

A self-assessment instrument, called Element B (Schutz, 1987), provides insight into teachers' own behavior as adults in a school environment. This instrument helps teachers determine where they are now (as opposed to where they want to be) in three behavior dimensions, *inclusion, control,* and *openness.*

The dimension of inclusion gives teachers information on how comfortable they are about having contact with others (in terms of working alone or working with others). The control dimension gives teachers insight into the degree of influence they prefer in setting others' direction. Finally, the openness dimension reveals how comfortable teachers are disclosing their feelings and thoughts and how open they are to listening to the feelings and thoughts of others. As trainers, we observe mixed reactions to this self-analysis. One teacher shared her feelings about her assessment: "I am not a real open person, but people come to me with their problems and concerns, and I listen."

The Philosophy of Education Inventory (Zinn, 1992) is an instrument that provides experienced teachers with an assessment of their own educational philosophy. An understanding of the diverse philosophies of a school's various teachers affects the school's teaching and learning environment and how its teacher leaders learn to communicate with others. For example, teachers who build their instruction around a humanist philosophy, which regards student interest as a key factor in curriculum planning, may have difficulty team teaching with teachers who favor a behaviorist philosophy, which takes a more structured approach to learning. Until teachers are clear about their own underlying teaching philosophy and understand the basis of other approaches, there can be conflict in working with other teachers.

Another personal assessment activity engages teachers in examining their values in the workplace. Teachers prioritize their own professional values and analyze the values that are evidenced in their schools' culture. A lack of congruence between a teacher's values and those of his or her school can account for discomfort in the workplace. If confronted with a significant gap, teachers may begin to consider other options.

Changing schools

Every teacher is influenced by the change process, either knowingly or unconsciously. Understanding how organizations change and what skills are necessary to move schools in a positive direction helps teacher leaders be more effective. From the research on why school change has failed, we have learned that there are predictable stages of change that have often been ignored. During LDT training, teachers discuss recent school innovations and apply their knowledge about change so that they can plan for these predictable stages in the future, to ensure success.

Moving beyond the classroom requires teachers to interact with other adults in group meetings. The development of these skills are of paramount importance as teachers influence change in their schools. Teachers engage in new leadership roles as recorders, reporters, and facilitators within groups. We often observe reluctance to practice these roles; however, in a risk-free environment, once the first fears are overcome the teachers use these roles with more self-assurance.

Teachers also assess their own school in relation to seven dimensions necessary to support teacher leadership. These dimensions, measured by the Teacher Leadership School Survey (Professional Development Center, 1991) are as follows:

- *Developmental focus*. Teachers are supported in learning new knowledge and skills and are encouraged to facilitate the learning of others.
- *Recognition*. Teachers are respected and recognized for their professional roles and the contributions they make.
- *Autonomy*. Teachers are encouraged to take the initiative in making improvements.
- *Collegiality*. Teachers collaborate on instructional and student-related matters.
- *Participation*. Teachers are actively involved in making decisions and have input on important matters.
- *Open communication*. Teachers send and receive communications in open and honest ways at their school.
- *Positive environment*. Teachers experience a positive climate and effective administrative leadership.

After scoring the instrument, teachers complete a graphic profile of their school. We encourage teachers to share their profiles with other teachers from their school and with teachers from other schools. In a group activity, teachers share their school's best practices in each dimension. Teachers collect strategies to take back to their school to help it build a stronger culture for teacher leadership.

Influencing strategies

Teachers taking on a leadership role know that they lack positional authority to influence others. For this reason it is important that they learn communication skills to work with their colleagues. This component sets the stage for teachers to practice and receive feedback on their influencing skills. After three days of activities in group settings, the teachers are ready on the fourth day for the influencing activities. The value of diversity in enhancing team relationships is stressed, and teachers use the knowledge they gained through the personal assessment component to understand diversity. A "new understanding" develops on how to communicate, using effective listening and influencing the strategies of others with diverse perspectives. Also, teachers strengthen their ability to use data to support their position and to reach agreement on current school issues. Observing a simulated school improvement meeting in which the teachers practiced influencing strategies, a visiting elementary principal commented, "Every principal should see this. They would feel a whole lot better about school improvement."

Planning for action

This component pulls together all of the essential pieces of the LDT program. It answers the question, "What can I do"? This question is necessary for teachers to prepare for reentry into their school environment. Teacher leadership transformation is evident when teachers prepare plans with specific, prioritized actions that can be used in their schools. Teachers share concerns and gain suggestions from peer participants. Teachers participate in a "back at school" problem-solving session, in which teams focus on work situations and plan how to influence change in their schools. One of the most rewarding activities for us is when teachers individually share their personalized action plans on the last day of training.

Follow-up support

Leaving a training program, teachers feel energized to influence change in their schools. Our concern has always been how effective these teachers will be as they reenter a school culture that may or may not embrace teacher leaders. Several strategies are built into the program to provide follow-up. Six months after their training, journal partners exchange letters highlighting their successes. This provides a timely follow-up and helps teachers assess their progress. The regional networks schedule reunions, which offer teacher leaders the opportunity to share success stories, reflect on their accomplishments, and review and practice their leadership skills. They collaborate and cooperatively work on real-life problems that they bring from their schools. Another strategy for follow-up is the dissemination of the *LDT Voice*, a teacher leadership newsletter. The newsletter helps teachers network by sharing a calendar of events, leadership tips, classroom innovations, and professional development programs.

Evidence of teacher leadership

After working with the program for a couple of years, we wanted to determine how teacher leadership was emerging. We collected data over a two-year period from LDT program participants to examine how teachers were influencing school change and what problems they were facing (Hart, Lewandowski, Segesta, and Bane, 1995).

Teachers' perceptions

During the 1993–94 school year, a survey was developed and distributed to teachers who had completed the training program. The purpose of the survey was to collect data relevant to the perceived impact of the training in the following three areas: career and professional development, personal and self-development, and workplace and work behaviors. A pattern emerged showing that at least 83 percent of the participants perceived a positive impact in each of the three areas. Some specific ways in which teachers felt their behavior had changed included feeling more comfortable expressing why they agreed or disagreed with something, listening to colleagues better, developing a better relationship with coworkers, and feeling more confident.

In another survey that same year, LDT participants were asked if they had influenced change in their school. Most teacher leaders told us that they had initiated programs or one-time events since completing the program. Examples of changes affecting students included organizing a schoolwide program on nonviolence, hosting a one-day conference on writing skills, offering parenting classes in the community, making monthly presentations about teaching strategies, and organizing multicultural field trips for students. Other teachers reported that they influenced changes in schools in the following ways: organizing instructional groups, devising new ways to involve exceptional students in regular classrooms, trying a different approach to reading instruction, and developing in-service plans to address the needs of students. Still other teacher leaders shared how they directly influenced subject area supervisors and (most of all) principals in their collaborative efforts to improve schools.

In the 1994–95 school year a survey was mailed to nine hundred additional teachers. Teachers who had received leadership training reported that they were applying these skills in their work and personal lives. They shared that they are now better listeners, communicators, and collaborators. One technology teacher said he had accomplished a years' worth of work in two and a half months using his newfound skills. He said, "It has taken all of the leadership skills I could muster to do this. We have had to deal with committees and teams, difficult-to-convince teachers, misinformation, and other assorted challenges. We met with success and are moving forward."

Teachers have reported to us that the roles of facilitator, reporter, and recorder have significantly changed their style of working with groups to address potential school problems. They feel that meetings are run more effectively and efficiently when they use these roles. By using these leadership roles, teachers feel that they can accomplish changes with greater ease and expertise.

Two teachers shared how they had practiced the facilitator's role. A third-grade teacher said he "used the skills to help build consensus on committees dealing with attendance, discipline, and technology issues. Also, the teachers have taken the initiative to correct deficiencies and are working together much better." Another teacher used her facilitation skills to train the entire staff at her school in conflict management. In addition, she trained over thirty students to be mediators.

Data were also collected during telephone interviews. Teachers who had completed the training reported becoming more influential through the use of good listening techniques, positive self-presentation, and newly acquired confidence in assuming leadership roles. The information documented in the telephone interviews indicated that teacher leaders used the skills stressed in the program.

Perceptions of others

Another facet of the evaluation was to conduct telephone interviews with colleagues of these teachers and their school administrators. Rather than relying solely on self-reports, these individuals could give information from different perspectives. The interviews focused on these individuals' perceptions of what skills and characteristics were exhibited by the teachers who had participated in the program (between 1991 and 1995).

Administrators identified problem solving as the most important skill exhibited by these teacher leaders. This was followed by having a vision, being dependable, having interpersonal skills, generating ideas, and being organizationally adept. An example of a principal's response was, "She is willing to take risks. She has tried new things. She does research. She looks for new ways to solve problems. She regroups and rearranges constantly." Similarly, principals describing these teachers commented that they "listen better," "help people draw themselves out," and "get people to buy in" to projects and school innovation. These responses may reflect teacher leaders' ability to help lighten the workload in their school.

The teachers' colleagues were more descriptive of the leadership examples than even the teacher participants themselves. Their colleagues perceived the teachers as leaders in developing new programs, writing grants, involving themselves and others, bringing new instructional ideas to others, and participating more than in the past. Colleagues also perceived the teachers as giving motivational and emotional support, facilitating school improvement teams, and training other teachers. One colleague described a teacher leader this way: "She has always been successful first with students. She seems to know what she is doing and how to approach things in a quiet and supportive, dependable, and enthusiastic way. She is really innovative as she tries new things."

Trainers' perspectives

As trainers in the LDT program, we also witness the professional growth of teachers. It is rewarding to observe the improvement teachers experience in specific skills and to hear them reflect on how they might apply these skills in their teaching practice. As one teacher put it, "I am no longer sitting back." These teacher leaders have also used their new skills at home, in church, and in civic activities. They also tell us that they have made perceptual shifts in how they understand others and that they use that ability to assist others. One teacher reflected that "It [the program] helped me personally in seeing myself and those around me differently."

During one of our sessions, five teachers from a local elementary school were participating in the program. On the evening of the third day, one of the teachers had to make a presentation to her school board that involved requesting funds for technology. The teacher used several strategies that she had practiced in the training program. The presentation was a success, and the school board approved her request. All of the teachers from her school were "riding on clouds" the following day. A group of high school teachers worked with their administrators to improve communication across all departments in the school by initiating and facilitating ten-minute brainstorming sessions during every class period. This gave small faculty groups a voice in addressing some of their concerns. They found a creative, efficient, and effective way to communicate and accomplish tasks. Another teacher transferred to a new school after she went through the training program. She reported that she had acquired a different outlook on her role as a teacher. She said, "I now get involved in all activities and give my viewpoint on topics and feel that I make a difference. I don't feel threatened by my peers and give it my best shot."

Teacher leadership in action

Teachers are emerging as leaders as they influence the development of improvement plans. Their leadership on school improvement teams has focused on student learning. In our 1994 evaluation, participants from the LDT program identified that they were responsible for over 167 different leadership roles in their schools.

Approximately 41 percent of the teachers surveyed were members of their school improvement teams, and 38 percent held a department or team leader position. Other roles included membership on school advisory councils and committee chairmanships for special school projects. There was a trend within districts to use teacher leaders on district task forces in all areas of curriculum, instruction, and staff development.

Another example of the emergence of teachers as leaders can be seen in a large school district where teachers serve as "collegial coaches" in each of the schools. The collegial coaches assist other teachers with professional development and help facilitate curriculum and program changes within the school. After completing the training program, they have periodic reunions to support one another as they implement their leadership skills. In another school district, 150 teachers have been selected as lead teachers in their schools during the 1995–96 school year. The district made a commitment to provide additional training for these teachers. The teachers commented on how the skills they learned in the LDT program have helped them in their position.

Supporting leadership development

It is evident from our experience and from the data from our participants and colleagues that teacher leadership is emerging in our state. This progress has not come without problems. Most of the issues revolve around the question "What's next?" The LDT program is only a five-day workshop; after the teachers leave, the real work begins. Although the program helps teachers develop an awareness of teacher leadership and offers them a chance to build leadership skills, it is up to the teachers to use these skills in their schools.

The context in which teachers approach leadership is critical to their success. The type of support they receive can determine their ability to be effective as leaders. In our work with teacher leaders, we have found that the barriers to establishing this kind of support need attention.

"Support" was described by the interviewees in our study in terms of interpersonal support, tangible support, or enlarged opportunities (Hart, Lewandowski, Segesta, and Bane, 1995). Interpersonal support consisted of approval from colleagues, recognition, and access to information (granted by administrators). Tangible support involved investment of fiscal resources, such as hiring substitute teachers for class coverage and paying for conferences. Enlarged opportunities offered teacher leaders expanded responsibilities. The teacher leaders, their colleagues, and administrators all cited examples of these types of support. The absence of these types of support hinders leadership work.

A dilemma arises when teacher leaders are successful. The natural tendency of administrators, and even the teachers themselves, is to expect successful teacher leaders to take on additional roles, usually without eliminating other responsibilities. The result is overload—teacher leaders trying to accomplish too much with too few resources.

Time

Finding time for training and leadership tasks is difficult when teachers are expected to be with their students at all times. For example, five days for training is a significant amount of time for teachers. Moreover, those teachers who volunteer to attend LDT training are usually the busiest teachers in their school. They are frequently out of their classrooms working on school improvement projects. It is difficult for them to find the time to attend training for their own skill development. We can count on long lines at the telephone during breaks, when these teachers check on their students back at their school. Time spent preparing to leave the classroom, in the training sessions themselves, and on follow-up when they return all take a toll on teacher leaders.

Principal reinforcement

Principals are supportive of the teachers attending the training program (otherwise they would not have provided the resources to have substitute teachers cover their classrooms). But after the teacher leaders return to their school, there is still need for support from the principal. The day-to-day press of school life interferes with principals' best intentions to meet with teacher leaders when they return. Unless the teacher is assertive, contact between principal and training participant may remain minimal. Our state has not developed a systematic approach for helping principals understand their role in reinforcing the leadership skills of their teachers.

Who is a teacher leader?

LDT program participants volunteer to attend on their own or through the encouragement of their principal. Most people still define teacher leaders in terms of traditional, formal roles such as department chairperson. Until there is an awareness that all teachers can assume leadership responsibilities, we will continue to attract only those who want to be formal leaders. We hope in the future that there will be expanded opportunities to invite more potential and informal teacher leaders to participate.

Conclusion

We are convinced that lifelong learning by teacher leaders in a school environment has more to do with school improvement than any accountability legislation. The LDT program is one approach to professional development for teacher leaders, with specific strategies to influence statewide systemic change in Florida. We are beginning to reap the benefits of providing leadership development experiences for our teachers. The primary benefit is that we are recognizing teacher leadership as a resource for the schools and for the teachers' own professional and personal development.

References

Hart, P., Lewandowski, A., Segesta, J., and Bane, M. *Evaluation of Leadership Development for Teachers.* Tampa, Fla.: West Central Educational Leadership Network, 1995.

Professional Development Center. *Teacher Leadership School Survey.* Plantation, Fla.: Professional Development Center, 1991.
Schutz, W. *Element B.* Mill Valley, Calif.: WSA, 1987.
Zinn, L. M. *Philosophy of Education Inventory.* Boulder, Colo.: Lifelong Learning Options, 1992.

PAMELA HART *is regional training coordinator at the West Central Educational Leadership Network, Tampa, Florida.*

BRUCE BAPTIST *is president of Pinellas Private Industry Council, Clearwater, Florida.*

This chapter gives readers a first-hand look at how teacher involvement in a school-based innovation can result in the emergence of teacher leadership. The authors provide a case study of a school team's work to improve student discipline using Total Quality Management. Teacher leadership evolved from teachers' involvement in the planning, use, and governance of the innovation. Key teacher leader characteristics are drawn from the project data. From their current perspectives as principals, the authors analyze the formal, informal, and potential leadership roles of teachers and clarify the importance of the principal's role in fostering teacher leaders.

6

Emergent teacher leaders

Joanne Warren Harrison, Emily Lembeck

NO ONE INDIVIDUAL has all the skills, knowledge, ideas, and time to carry out all the complex tasks involved in school improvement (Gardner, 1990). As principals, we are bombarded daily with demands and suggestions for school reform. By virtue of our position, our constituents presume that we hold the sole power to effect change and guarantee school improvement; however, as schools have become larger and more complex, we realize this is simply not possible. Therefore, schools have begun replacing their outmoded bureaucratic educational structures with shared leadership models.

Even though we are from different states with different school populations, we share a common belief that teacher leadership plays a critical role in implementing shared leadership. Over the past few years, we have spent hours together discussing the definition of

NEW DIRECTIONS FOR SCHOOL LEADERSHIP, NO. 1, FALL 1996 ©JOSSEY-BASS PUBLISHERS teacher leadership, the development of teacher leaders, and the informal and formal roles they assume in our schools. Based on our shared experiences, research, and readings, we characterize teacher leaders as individuals who are actively involved in promoting change, effectively communicate with multiple constituents, possess a global understanding of school and district organizations, and continue to grow professionally.

We agree that to develop these qualities teachers need training, time, knowledge, and team-building experiences. We also recognize that teacher leaders cannot develop without consistent support and encouragement from their principal. Support from those persons in positions of power is of immeasurable value in bringing about change and developing future leaders (Maeroff, 1993).

This chapter describes a project designed to involve teachers in setting up programs to improve student discipline by developing students' social skills. This initiative, intended to improve student behavior, produced an unexpected by-product: the emergence of teachers as leaders.

Context

In this chapter we analyze the experience one of us had as a teacher leader in Lakeside Elementary School's improvement initiative (Lembeck, 1995) from our current perspective as elementary school principals. We then examine the issues surrounding the emergence of teacher leadership. Next we offer suggestions for developing teachers as leaders and insights about identifying teacher leaders. From the study of the work at Lakeside Elementary, we list key attributes of teacher leaders.

Background

A midsize suburban school district, historically considered an innovator in education, came under public criticism for its declining test scores and unsuccessful restructuring efforts. In response to this criticism, the system's top leaders began to investigate Total Quality Management (TQM) as a means of effecting change. The school district mandated each school to form a school-based TQM project team.

The student population at Lakeside Elementary School is representative of the district's socioeconomic and racial diversity. The students come from a variety of home environments and possess a wide range of abilities. The school had 502 students enrolled at the time of the study. The principal was halfway through her second year; the previous principal had been at the school for eighteen years. Throughout the previous administrator's tenure, the faculty had remained stable, with little personnel change.

The Lakeside Elementary TQM project team consisted of ten members. All members were female, held advanced degrees in education, and had been professional educators for more than seven years. One was black, one was Hispanic, and the rest were white. Each of the members had agreed to serve on the team.

Structure

As a first step toward improving student discipline, the team selected the development of a social skills program as its focus for a TQM initiative. Training for this project consisted of four sessions with a TQM consultant. Classroom teachers received release time to attend these off-campus training sessions.

The training sessions provided experience, knowledge, and guidance for problem solving using TQM processes. The first time the team met, the consultant provided an in-depth overview of TQM philosophy and its application to schools. Team-building activities were also part of this meeting and were subsequently included in all future training sessions. The second and third training sessions concentrated on data collection, problem solving, and planning.

The final TQM pilot team training session addressed three objectives. The first objective was to introduce new TQM tools for data collection and measurement. The consultant taught the team when and how to use checklists, Pareto charts, run charts, histograms, stem-leaf diagrams, affinity diagrams, and responsibility matrixes. Team members used a run chart to examine the progress of the social skills project over a specified period of time.

The second objective of the training was to expand the team's knowledge and understanding of the continuous improvement cycle, a central component of the TQM philosophy. Continuous improvement is principally achieved through an ongoing planning cycle known as PDCA (Plan, Do, Check, Act). Basically, the team makes a plan, implements it, checks the results (and makes changes if necessary), and acts to institutionalize the (refined) plan.

The final objective of the training involved the team's evaluating its own performance. During the self-evaluation activity, team members used an affinity diagram to generate data on the team's training. From these data the group identified effective team-building strategies as well as areas that needed improvement. A responsibility matrix was developed to ensure a realistic schedule of tasks to be completed by team members. In addition to the four training sessions, eight school-based meetings were held. Each meeting enabled team members to use their newly attained skills and develop their capacity to work productively as a team. An analysis of the minutes of the meetings revealed a sharing of ideas, open disagreement among members, and the capability of the group to reach consensus. As team members applied their new skills and tools, they experienced frustration, confusion, and excitement. After months, the TQM efforts resulted in the development of synergy among the team members.

Throughout the development of this project, team members continued to learn about TQM and social skills instruction. As the team became a learning community, they read and shared articles, then obtained and disseminated information to specific grade-level teachers and to the school staff as a whole. Team members also presented a synopsis of TQM's philosophy and reported on the project's progress at faculty meetings, to support staff, and to district-level personnel. In addition, team members practiced reflective writing as a means of professional development.

The actual implementation of the social skills project occurred toward the end of the school year. The team members regularly met to gather data and assess the effectiveness of the project. Post-project data was examined, and the next cycle of the TQM process of continuous improvement was planned for the coming year.

System changes

During the time the project was developed and implemented and the training occurred, there were several changes in leadership at the district level. After serving for twelve years, the superintendent left the system; the associate superintendent was named interim superintendent. The school board concentrated on finding a replacement for the superintendent, and this paralyzed the system. As other top leaders left the school district, along with them went the district's support for the TQM initiative.

The Lakeside Elementary project team started the school year unaware that the system's support for the TQM initiative had eroded. The members of team did not realize the impact that this change would have on the TQM initiative. As the school board named a new superintendent, the media pushed for an upgraded curriculum. Specifically, the media demanded that the schools cease experimenting with children and return to the basics. An anti-innovation cry from a concerned public was heard throughout the district. However, the political climate in the district appeared to have no immediate effect on the local schools' TQM initiative.

Two weeks after the new school year began, the Lakeside Elementary project team met to plan for the continuation of the social skills program. The next scheduled meeting was abruptly canceled by the principal, without an explanation to the team or faculty members. After this, there were no further project team meetings, nor were there discussions relating to TQM or the social skills project. Teachers began to question whether the project team would meet again. As time passed the unspoken message was that TQM had become a nonentity in the school and the system. At this point it was unknown if there were any lasting effects from the unsustained initiative.

Issues

As the project progressed, teacher leadership issues became evident. Addressing these issues can provide principals with an understanding of how they can support teacher leadership. Since the study was completed, we identified practices we use that assist teacher leaders.

Unanticipated emergence of teacher leadership

A research study was designed to evaluate TQM as vehicle for school improvement (Lembeck, 1995). The study was supposed to assess changes in student behavior, but the data gathered through interviews and reflective writings shifted the focus to changes in the attitudes and behaviors of teachers. This project, expressly developed to change student behavior, had actually changed teacher behavior. Surprisingly, team members spoke about the project's effects on themselves, not on their students. An attempt to refocus the questions back to the original purpose of the study proved futile. Teachers continued to share their new understanding of leadership and their new role as teacher leaders. For the first time, teachers on this project team viewed themselves as leaders.

It is widely recognized that the development of teacher leaders extends over a period of time (Pellicer and Anderson, 1995). In the early stages, emerging teacher leaders expand their roles and responsibilities; however, they often lack the confidence and experience to transfer their leadership skills to new situations. As we analyzed the collapse of this project, we realized that the teachers did not have the confidence, knowledge, or experience to continue the program without the support of the district or the principal. Since the principal was new to the school, a sufficient amount of trust had not yet developed to enable the teachers to feel they could question the administration or offer alternatives.

Principals' support

Principals' effectiveness has been associated with positive forms of influence (Blase and Kirby, 1992). From the onset of this project, the principal influenced the development of the teacher leaders. The selection of team members by the principal was an early and critical influence on the project's outcome. The teachers selected by the principal were respected by their colleagues, receptive to change, and eager to participate in the project.

Throughout the project, the principal's influence and support were evident. She provided release time for training and meetings, along with the necessary resources to ensure project success. Notable support was demonstrated as the principal stepped out of her formal role and became an equal member of the team. As one team member commented, "It is not just one leader. . . . It is everyone playing a role as leader—being part of a team." Throughout the project period, she continued to model the learning behaviors associated with the development of leadership. She attended conferences, read, researched, and shared her knowledge.

With the clearly articulated positions taken by the new superintendent, it was clear that TQM would no longer be a school system priority. Principals are acutely aware of the superintendent's posture toward school restructuring efforts and often gauge their efforts to coincide with their perception of the superintendent's support (Prestine and Bowen, 1993). Accordingly, the principal discontinued support for the TQM initiative. However, the knowledge and skills that had been gained were carried on in other school improvement efforts. Even though the TQM project was disbanded, the principal recognized the changes it had achieved in both the school's teachers and in the lines of communication established during this process. A leadership team was ultimately reinstated in the school, and the skills, process, and procedures learned during this project were reapplied to new opportunities. The collaborative spirit developed in the TQM project continues to exist in the school.

Developing teacher leaders

Even without district support a principal can create an environment that will enhance leadership in individuals. The principal must find ways to create structures to help teachers develop their thinking and behavior beyond the limits of their experience. From our perspective as principals who wish to develop teachers as leaders, we suggest the following for supporting this kind of development.

Providing release time. Teachers need time not only to work together but also to begin defining their own set of values and beliefs. The following are some of the strategies we have used in our schools:

- Have teachers raise money by performing in a teacher talent show. Use the money to hire substitute teachers, allowing grade-levels and content area committees and team leaders to meet during the school day.
- Provide common planning periods. Adjust classes to enable groups of teachers to collaborate on projects and planning.
- Have support staff cover classes during special programs to give teachers a block of time to work together.

Communicating. Teachers are comfortable speaking in front of their students, but they are often fearful of communicating ideas to an audience of adults. Strategies to consider include the following:

- Schedule faculty meetings by grade levels, in different classrooms. Have a host teacher provide a brief overview of each grade level's program.
- Use teachers' expertise in school-based staff development activities.
- Encourage teachers to facilitate schoolwide or committee meetings.
- Select teachers to represent the school at district and community meetings.

Developing staff. Teacher acquisition of new knowledge is essential to school reform. Self-awareness enables teachers to better understand themselves and their interactions with others. Approaches we have used include the following:

- Administer self-awareness inventories to teachers. Analyze the results and discuss their implications.

- Distribute professional articles to teachers.
- Organize study groups on specific topics.
- Train teachers in each grade level to become experts in a content area. These teachers can then serve as valuable resources to others.
- Send teachers to national conferences or workshops. In many cases businesses will assist with funding.

Building leadership skills. To function as leaders, teachers need the skills necessary to create agendas, facilitate meetings, implement projects, and promote leadership in others. Ways to accomplish this include the following:

- Procure outside consultants to train teacher leaders.
- Offer programs that teach the skills necessary to effectively conduct meetings.
- Have principals demonstrate, model, and discuss strategies that teacher leaders can incorporate into their daily routine or curriculum.
- Ask principals to informally mentor teacher leaders. Visit potential teacher leaders during their planning periods or after school. Create a relaxed environment that will foster open lines of communication. Encourage discussion about their new roles.
- Provide classroom coverage so teachers can shadow administrators. During the shadowing experience, periodically discuss the teacher's observations.
- Delegate responsibility for projects. Provide structures for success, such as time lines, explicit directions, and resources. Ongoing encouragement is needed.

Building teams. Teachers need to be able to collaborate, reach a consensus, and work together productively. We suggest the following techniques:

- Informal team building can begin at social functions outside school or at regular faculty meetings. Have teachers sit with different groups of teachers. This can be accomplished by giving teachers different types of candy as they enter the meeting; teachers with same type of candy sit together.

- Train teachers on team-building skills such as brainstorming and consensus building, decision-making skills, and problem-solving strategies.

Acknowledging teachers as leaders. We have learned several ways to acknowledge teacher leadership. To develop a culture that recognizes this new role for teachers, we propose the following steps:

- Set up the expectation that all teachers will be leaders. At the beginning of each school year, ask teachers to identify and commit to leadership tasks in the school. Allow new teachers and those learning new procedures to opt out of leadership responsibilities for the year.
- Expand the role of the teacher in the organization. Teachers must not just be responsible for the students they teach; they must become an integral part of schoolwide decision-making processes. After receiving the appropriate training, invite teachers to participate in decision making, especially in areas directly related to classroom instruction.
- Recognize teachers' expertise. Teachers are rarely seen as experts in their own building. Provide forums for teachers to share their ideas and demonstrate their knowledge. This can be accomplished through teacher fairs where teachers display successful projects and conduct mini workshops. This type of activity could culminate in a celebration.
- Distinguish teacher leaders as professionals. Schedule off-campus release time for planning and staff development. Highlight at least one instance of success at every faculty meeting. Recognize teachers' accomplishments in public forums and through the media. Send individual notes that specifically acknowledge their professionalism. Honor teachers of the year by displaying their picture, giving them a special parking spot, introducing them at all functions, and spotlighting their talents.

The principal's role

Just as the teachers in this study redefined their roles to include leadership, so must the school principal think differently about his or her role. Principals must strive to become leaders of leaders. They must build the capacity of teachers and others so that direct supervision of them can be minimized.

Principals must also serve as guides, providing support throughout the development process. As stated by one of the project team members, "The principal serves as a guide—leading but not directing, supporting new ways of thinking, and providing opportunities for professional growth." Teachers must be organized, mobilized, and led and nurtured by supportive and concerned principals (Lieberman, 1988a).

Principals need to create a culture that recognizes the skills and expertise of teachers. Finding ways to celebrate and reward those who accept leadership roles in their school is a challenge. Principals must identify meaningful ways to reward teachers in ways teachers value. The creation of a school culture that celebrates teacher leadership will foster the identification of future leaders.

Identifying teacher leaders

As we grow as leaders, we begin to recognize leadership in others. Teacher leaders in our schools fall into three categories: formal, informal, and potential teacher leaders.

Formal teacher leaders have been selected by the administration or by colleagues to be chairpersons or grade-level representatives. In addition, these individuals often represent the school and the principal at district meetings or serve on district committees. To satisfy their own desire for learning, these teachers are continuous learners, improving their knowledge and practice.

In every school there are those teachers who have distinguished themselves from their peers by assuming *informal* leadership roles. These teachers are committed not only to their own practices but also to the profession as a whole. They define success in terms of what happens in the entire school, not just their classrooms.

These leaders are recognized by peers and administrators as those staff members who are always volunteering to head new projects, mentor and support other teachers, accept responsibility for their own professional growth, introduce new ideas, and promote the mission of the school.

Potential teacher leaders are those individuals who explore the possibility of what could be rather than remaining entrenched in what is. As they grow, they include new ideas and techniques in their practice. In short, they step beyond their own comfort level to enhance the classroom and school programs.

Principals seeking to identify potential leadership in teachers should first observe grade-level and committee meetings. During these observations, principals should begin to take note of those teachers who are active listeners, are team players, are well organized, and evoke the respect of their colleagues. For all their strengths, these teachers do not view themselves as leaders.

Key attributes of teacher leaders

Further analysis of the project results revealed a list of attributes describing teacher leaders. These attributes matched the characteristics we had identified previously. As the attributes of teacher leadership are further clarified, we are better able to present examples of individuals emerging in the new role of teacher leader.

1. *Teacher leaders are actively involved in promoting change.* As we reviewed the project we recognized that teacher leaders are actively involved in promoting change. In this project, the teacher leaders worked to solve an important school problem through the use of TQM tools and processes. They researched, collected pertinent data, shared new concepts and existing programs, and took ownership of the problem at hand. As one teacher leader stated, "It was a very thorough way of analyzing a problem and getting to a solution rather than a quick fix. It made me think of the problem much more thoroughly." Overwhelmingly, the project team members

enjoyed working as a team and developed confidence in group processes. They became comfortable with the development and expression of possibilities. Based on their newly acquired skills and confidence, the team members served as a catalyst for schoolwide change.

2. *Teacher leaders can effectively communicate with multiple constituents.* It became evident that the members of the project team communicated with a number of different constituents. As noted, they became liaisons between the TQM project team and classroom teachers. At grade-level meetings, the teacher leaders promoted change as they facilitated the group process. According to one team member, "We were responsible for going back to our grade-level teams . . . not to train them but to explain the process thoroughly and to work with the process so that they felt a part of it." A survey completed by classroom teachers confirmed this finding. Teachers reported that they were extremely satisfied with the communication they received from the project team. Furthermore, classroom teachers believed that because of the team's efforts to involve the staff in the project, instructional time was protected. The teacher leaders also gave presentations about the project at faculty, support personnel, and district-level meetings.

In addition to newly acquired group presentation skills, a new form of communication was established between the team and the principal. Ongoing dialogue replaced top-down directives. The initial training session enabled all team members, including the principal, to develop positive and productive team behaviors. These behaviors, with clarified roles and an emphasis on valued communication, carried over into school-based meetings and into the decision-making process. Teacher leaders acknowledged the importance of communication not only within the school but also with parents and the school community. Therefore, the teacher leaders ensured that information about the project was communicated through grade-level and schoolwide newsletters.

3. *Teacher leaders possess a global understanding of school and district organization.* Project team members gained a new understanding of school and school district operations. As the project

unfolded, the team members became aware of the impact their ideas and recommendations had on the school. Specifically, the team members needed release time in order to plan and implement the project. For the first time, teacher leaders examined the variables in scheduling and planning. This problem forced the team members to look beyond the four walls of their classroom for viable solutions. As one of the new teacher leaders stated, "I never knew what it took to arrange class coverage and how many people it involved." The more teachers share leadership, responsibility, and accountability with one another and the principal, the more they come to perceive the school as a community (Lieberman, 1988b)

The project's demise caused the team members to examine the district's politics. Each member reported in some manner that TQM was not a part of the new superintendent's agenda. The members perceived that the principal did not have the authority to continue the project without the superintendent's endorsement. The teacher leaders gained insight into the complex organization governing their school. They accepted as fact that their site leader could not continue a publicly unpopular innovation without the support of the superintendent.

4. *Teacher leaders continue to grow professionally.* When the TQM project team members wrote reflectively about their experience, they all stated that they had grown as professionals. The majority of the teacher leaders reported that they had become more confident. This, we believe, is the result of their active participation in promoting change, effective communication with multiple constituents, and global understanding of their school and district organizations. This new confidence was echoed in the feelings of pride the participants expressed about their involvement with the project. "Opportunity," "excited," "elite," and "privileged" were descriptors used in interviews and reflective writings.

Furthermore, all project team members experienced a change in their beliefs about leadership. As a result, they assumed new professional roles and responsibilities. These new roles and responsibilities called for new attitudes about change, communication, professional growth, and school organization. As one member summarized it, "My beliefs changed about the role of leadership. I never looked at myself in a leadership role—I now have the confidence in my ability. I see myself and all teachers as potential leaders in the school."

Clearly, the new teacher leaders equated the training with professionalism. A majority of the team members emphasized the training aspect of the TQM experience as a means of professional development. As one team member reflected, "I am appreciative of the respect given me by the district in that they offered me this training and sought my input into this process. It certainly makes me feel professional."

Anticipating the emergence of teacher leaders

Teacher leaders evolve from being teachers of students, to teachers of teachers, to leaders of teachers. Principals do not have to wait for the unexpected emergence of teacher leaders. They can identify potential teacher leaders and promote their development. We have offered insights and recommendations on the development of teacher leaders based on our experiences as principals.

To begin this process is to challenge basic assumptions about teachers. Based on the assumption that teachers are indeed leaders, principals can test their intentions by asking themselves these questions:

- Am I willing to alter the organizational structure of my school to support teachers as leaders?
- Am I prepared to relinquish power to teacher leaders?
- Will I shift resources in order to supply the necessary training and support?
- Can I declare that I am a leader of leaders?

Principals who can answer these questions affirmatively are committed to the development of teacher leaders. We believe that principals can anticipate the emergence of teacher leaders if they are truly committed to their development. As teacher leaders emerge, so do the answers for school improvement.

References

Blase, J., and Kirby, P. C. *Bringing Out the Best in Teachers: What Effective Principals Do.* Newbury Park, Calif.: Corwin Press, 1992.

Gardner, J. W. *On Leadership.* New York: Free Press, 1990.

Lembeck, E. "Total Quality Management: One School's Tools for Change." Unpublished doctoral dissertation, University of Georgia, Athens, 1995.

Lieberman, A. "Expanding the Leadership Team." *Educational Leadership*, 1988a, *45*(5), 18–21.

Lieberman, A. "Teachers and Principals: Turf, Tension, and New Tasks." *Phi Delta Kappan*, 1988b, *5*, 12–17.

Maeroff, G. I. *Team Building for School Change: Equipping Teachers for New Roles.* New York: Teachers College Press, 1993.

Pellicer, L. O., and Anderson, L. W. *A Handbook for Teacher Leaders.* Thousand Oaks, Calif.: Corwin Press, 1995.

Prestine, N. A., and Bowen, C. "Benchmarks of Change: Assessing Essential School Restructuring Efforts. *Education Evaluation & Policy Analysis*, 1993, *15*(3), 298–319.

JOANNE WARREN HARRISON *is principal of Palm Cove Elementary School in Pembroke Pines, Florida.*

EMILY LEMBECK *was a teacher leader at Lakeside Elementary School and is now principal of Dunleith Elementary School in Marietta, Georgia.*

A teacher leader and a district administrator from a large urban school district look at the transformation of teachers into leaders. The teachers described in this chapter moved beyond their classrooms to examine instructional practices with teachers in other schools within a feeder pattern. Collaboration among the teachers centered on teaching and learning. Project participants evolved from successful teachers to strong instructional leaders, as perceived by their school and the district. The authors describe the leadership skills developed by these teachers as well as other leadership responsibilities they assumed.

7

SUNRAYS:
Cultivating teacher leaders
in an urban community

Billy F. Birnie, Casey Lustgarten

IMAGINE A FIELD PLOWED, planted, and watered. The soil is rich, the seeds fertile, the water plentiful. The potential crop lies dormant until the sun shines. It is the *sun's rays* that give warmth and light to the tiny seeds, causing them to develop, flourish, and yield a rich harvest.

In the inner city of Miami, eleven schools make up a feeder pattern. (A "feeder pattern" is formed by the elementary, middle, and high schools that share the same students; in this case, eight elementary schools and two middle schools feed into the senior high school.) Two years ago, those schools were like the field described above: the potential was in them; that is, they were staffed

NEW DIRECTIONS FOR SCHOOL LEADERSHIP, NO. 1, FALL 1996 © JOSSEY-BASS PUBLISHERS

with teachers poised and ready to work for positive change. What was missing was the "sun's rays," the avenue for tapping that potential and turning it into constructive leadership that would result in higher student achievement, stronger professional commitment, and more nurturing learning environments for both children and adults.

The eleven principals had already demonstrated their capacity to work effectively as a team. In fact, just the year before, in 1992–93, they had launched a feeder pattern initiative to train and coach teams of teachers in their schools. It was called Project RAISE, for Raising Achievement by Increasing Student Expectations. At the end of the 1992–93 school year, it was clear that Project RAISE needed to continue—but the principals wanted more for their schools than Project RAISE could deliver. So they embarked upon a second feeder pattern project, called "Son of RAISE" in jest and then officially named SUNRAYS, in part to maintain its "genealogy" and in part to reflect the principals' expectations for what this new project would do: nurture the growth of every teacher in their schools and then improve the academic performance of their students. They envisioned teams of teachers from their own faculties visiting all of the schools in the feeder pattern, reporting on their observations, and bringing home new ideas for making teaching and learning more effective. SUNRAYS was thus subtitled "A Project for Disseminating Best Practices in a Community of Schools," and a sun with rays emanating from it was chosen as its logo.

We were involved in this exciting adventure right from the start, Billy as the designer and director of the project and Casey as one of the teachers chosen to participate as a team member. Along with others involved with the project, we have seen SUNRAYS not only accomplish what it set out to do but also produce a cadre of teacher leaders whose own growth and development have astonished all of us.

What follows is the story of SUNRAYS: a brief description of each component in the project's design, with elaboration on the site visit; an account of the transformation of the team members; a description of the project's benefits; and essential considerations for the project's implementation. The story is told with two kinds of readers in mind: those who are interested in obtaining the same or similar benefits in their schools by implementing or adapting SUN-RAYS, and those who are interested in gleaning information about the conditions that cultivate teacher leaders in schools.

Project design

The project includes these components: team member selection, identification of indicators of best practices, orientation of school staffs, preparation for peer observations, site visits, written follow-up, collection of examples of best practices, debriefing, and evaluation (see Figure 7.1).

Team member selection

Each principal selected two teachers, choosing teachers who were admired by their peers and were willing to take risks. In fact, some of the twenty-two teachers came to the first briefing on blind faith in their principals' judgment, knowing nothing of what would be expected of them. Those twenty-two teachers continued to serve on the project (except for the rare exceptions who moved out of the community) until the third year, when some principals chose to rotate one of their two team members in order to give another teacher an opportunity to learn and grow.

Identification of indicators of best practices

During the first full-day briefing, team members realized that their mission was to identify and disseminate best teaching practices. The teachers agreed that the first task was to create a description of what those practices are. So, drawing from their own experience and knowledge of current research as well as that of district subject area specialists who joined them for the initial session, the teachers

Figure 7.1. SUNRAYS Project Design.

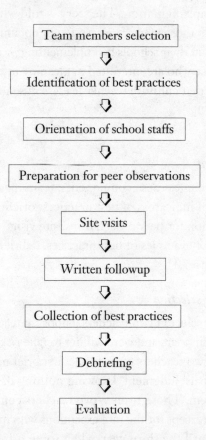

constructed a list of "indicators" of best teaching practices. Items on the list ranged from specific strategies, such as "The teacher reads aloud to students daily," to more generic behaviors, such as "Instruction is designed and delivered so that it meets the needs of all students, including those with diverse linguistic backgrounds and those with special needs." Elementary school practices were categorized by total school environment, language arts, mathematics, science, and social studies. Secondary practices included total school environment and classroom practices. Together, these indicators of best practices make up the checklist that teachers now use as a basis for making observations during site visits.

Orientation of school staffs and preparation for peer observations

In the first year, a second full-day briefing for team members was devoted to two tasks: drafting a letter to teachers in the schools to be visited and preparing team members for what many of them viewed as the daunting challenge of observing other teachers' classes.

The letter team members wrote to their peers whose classrooms they would be visiting emphasized these points:

1. This is a cooperative project, one that administrators and teachers requested and not a region, district, or state mandate.
2. It is a supportive project, intended to showcase, celebrate, and replicate the good things happening in our schools.
3. Conversely, it is not evaluative or judgmental. We will not visit your classroom to evaluate, judge, or criticize.
4. We are your peers and colleagues, not your superiors. We look forward to strengthening the communications network among teachers in our feeder pattern.
5. At the closing meeting on the day we visit your school, we will give you positive feedback on the good things we have seen and some recommendations that may help you continue to improve your school's teaching and learning environment.
6. The SUNRAYS project is ongoing, and its success depends on continued networking, peer visits to classrooms, and increased attention to the indicators of best practices that will improve student achievement.

Preparation of team members for observations focused on techniques for alleviating anxiety in the teachers to be observed (and in the observers!), clinical observation skills, attention to the indicators of best practices, and professional demeanor. Most of the team members had never observed other teachers' classes before, and surely not for the purpose of giving feedback to their peers, so this training was an essential part of preparing them for taking the risks involved in becoming teacher leaders in classrooms other than their own.

Discussions centered on the subtle but critical cues that observers give to classroom teachers: a smile and body language that convey a friendly visit; questions that indicate genuine interest in what the teacher and students are doing; keen attention to the students' work, at their desks, in their folders and portfolios, in displays around the room; and spending enough time in each classroom to get an accurate perception of the instructional program. Attention was also given to the fine art of giving constructive feedback that focuses not on individual teachers but on a grade level's program—feedback that includes both praise for exemplary practices and suggestions that will assist teachers in building on their strengths.

Site visits

After those two days of orientation, the twenty-two teachers divided into two teams, the SUN Team and the RAYS Team. Each team included one teacher from each school. During the middle months of the school year (November to February), each team visited four elementary schools and one middle school, spending a whole day at each school. Then the two teams (all twenty-two teachers) joined forces to visit the senior high school, which, with an enrollment of nearly 2,800 and a teaching staff of about 140, required more visitors in order for all classes to be observed. The site visits, described in the following section, included observations of all of the core academic classes (language arts, mathematics, science, social studies) and most of the other classes as well. Each visit culminated with a report from team members to the school's faculty; all team members participated in delivering the report. Drafts of the reports, which contain praise for exemplary instructions, suggestions for improvement, and descriptions of creative teaching strategies observed, were submitted to the principal and to the team leader at the end of the day.

Written follow-up

After the visits, the written reports were typed and sent back to the school so that all teachers could have a copy either of the full report or of the segment that pertained to their subject or grade level. These reports are used as a basis for improving instruction from one year to the next, so much so, in fact, that in some schools, teachers have transformed last year's recommendations into this year's commendations. For example, last year at Van E. Blanton Elementary School, the RAYS team recommended securing more books for classroom libraries and making the school a more inviting place to learn. This year, two of the commendations were as follows:

1. Classrooms continue to be enriched with more trade books, working toward the goal of at least five to seven books per child in the classroom libraries.
2. The physical plant of the school has been upgraded so that the learning environment is more appealing and inviting to the staff, students, and community.

   Another example of a school that transformed recommendations into commendations was West Little River Elementary. Teachers continued the use of block scheduling to allow for effective common planning time and professional development. Teachers and students continued their efforts to prepare fourth-grade students for the state's writing assessment, and they provided evidence that there was schoolwide intra- and inter-grade planning and sharing among teachers to coordinate and integrate the district's competency-based curriculum. (One team member said of her own faculty after this year's visit, "They're really aiming to make all of the recommendations into commendations. They're asking, 'What can I do for next time?' That's *next year*—but they've already got a plan of action to improve from this point to take them through to next year, when the team comes back.")

Collection of examples of best practices

The written descriptions of creative teaching strategies observed are held until the end of the year, when they are compiled into a booklet and duplicated for every teacher in the feeder pattern. Here is an example from last year's booklet:

"Shadow—Who Am I?"
Using an overhead projector or a lamp that casts shadows on poster paper taped to the wall, outline the shadow of only the student's head and then cut it out, making a silhouette. Then have the students look through magazines and find pictures to represent their interests, feelings, family, etc. They may paste the pictures inside or around the silhouette and then write about what the collage represents.

Debriefing

After all of the site visits, team members meet again to debrief. A look backward gives them the opportunity to reflect on the work done in the schools and to analyze their own growth, and a look forward provides the chance to make recommendations and plan for the next year.

Evaluation

SUNRAYS is continually evaluated, informally by all of the teachers whose classes are observed during the year and formally by team members and principals, whose voices will be heard later in this chapter.

The heart of the project: the site visit

The schedule for a SUNRAYS site visit is as follows.

8:00 to 9:00 a.m. The team meets at the school with the principal, who discusses the master schedule, the school's improvement plan, and the time and place for the after-school meeting. The team leader assigns members to grade-level groups, designating a chair for each subteam. Each subteam is responsible for visiting all of the classes and teachers in its assigned grade and for writing and delivering the reports for the grade.

9:00 a.m. to 12:00 Noon. Subteams observe classes, using the indicators of best practices as a guide for their observations.

12:00 Noon to 1:00 p.m. The team convenes for lunch and a midday briefing.

1:00 to 2:30 p.m. Subteams continue observing classes, if time permits, and prepare reports, comments on the checklist, praise for observed examples of best practices, and recommendations for continued improvement. Exceptionally effective teaching strategies are written up for the booklet to be produced later, and "champions" (master teachers) are identified for the team leader so they may be tapped later as instructional leaders.

2:30 to 3:30 p.m. The team meets with the faculty and administration. The principal introduces the team leader, who greets the staff, reminds them of who we are and why we are here, and calls on each subteam to present their report. The "total school report" is delivered by the team leader, who shares findings that pertain to the entire instructional program. The meeting culminates with a conversation between the faculty and the team members about the status of teaching and learning in the school.

Transformation of teacher leaders

Both of us see a change in the teacher leaders involved in SUNRAYS. Although our roles are different, our perspectives are similar.

The teacher leader's perspective (Casey)

Three years ago, when SUNRAYS first began, as teachers we lacked confidence and experience in giving and receiving feedback, especially in unfamiliar classrooms and schools. We believed that we had minimal observational, listening, and influencing skills. We came from a variety of classrooms, backgrounds, and grade levels, and we brought widely divergent perceptions to our work. We had never been asked to observe strangers' classes, much less to forge those observations and differing opinions into positive, constructive written reports and then present our findings to a roomful of teachers we had never met. We were was frightened to stand in front of, much less speak to, a strange faculty. Over the past three years all of that has changed.

For me, being a member of SUNRAYS has helped me feel comfortable in a variety of settings, both inside and outside of my school. To begin with, inside my school, my role as Title I reading resource teacher blossomed, and my ability to assist in developing effective instructional lessons was enriched by my visits to other classrooms and schools. I was able to glean research-based strategies and share them with teachers in our school. My leadership positions within the school included being on the school improvement committee, being chairman of the achievement committee, being a member of the cadre for school-based management, being on the teacher-of-the-year selection committee, and being coordinator of many workshops for credit through our teacher education center (current examples include "Teachers as Readers" and "Portfolio Assessment" as well as numerous reading and writing workshops).

In addition to expanding my role inside the school, SUNRAYS has helped me feel comfortable in various settings outside the school as well. As my confidence and self-esteem grew, my willingness to take risks increased, allowing me to grow professionally. I participated in numerous workshops and developed language arts curricula for the district, the Title I office, our regional area, and individual schools. This year I presented, along with my fellow teachers, at the state's reading conference. Before SUNRAYS, I would have lacked the confidence and self-esteem to speak before an audience of knowledgeable administrators. Over the past year, I was appointed to a local university's advisory council, and I served as an adjunct instructor for the university's graduate students.

In the community, I serve as a board member on two charitable organizations. With all of these groups, I try to focus on the positive, not the negative, just as the SUNRAYS team does with their visits. SUNRAYS has made me less critical, more diplomatic, a careful observer and listener, and a person willing to go out and take risks in order to grow. I know from conversations with other SUNRAYS teachers that they have experienced the same kind of transformation.

The regional director's perspective (Billy)

I can vouch for what Casey says. I approached this project with enthusiasm and confidence, but that was not how the teachers felt at first, either during the briefings or the early site visits. I remember the looks on their faces in the first briefing when they heard their charge. Teaching their own classes was one thing; serving as eyes and ears for teachers they had never met was quite another. Their confidence grew, however, with the development of the indicators of best practices. As they hammered out the descriptors of teaching and learning, they were working with content they knew well; they were also learning more about one another and about how to talk, listen, and write together—skills that would serve them well during the site visits, and indeed, during the rest of their careers.

The first site visit of the RAYS Team is etched indelibly in my mind. We visited Miami Park Elementary School, with an enrollment approaching 1,200 and thus almost one hundred teachers. The morning session went well, and the observations were novel and stimulating for team members. Writing the reports presented some challenges, but that task, too, was completed with relatively little stress. It was the after-school meeting that struck me with the image of "growth in progress." Team members fidgeted as they watched the teachers file into the cavernous cafeteria and settle down. The acoustics are poor there, so we used a microphone, one more intimidation for novice speakers. As the team members walked to the front of the room, I wasn't sure that some of them might not head for the exit door instead of the podium. Fortunately, they had their reports in writing; many of them read to the vast audience, and I noticed trembling knees beneath more than one skirt as reports were made.

When I compare that day to our most recent visit, the contrast is startling. The whole team—twenty-two teachers—arrived at

Miami Central Senior High School on a spring morning, greeting each other warmly in the parking lot and meeting room, exchanging the latest news—personal and professional, for these teachers are friends as well as colleagues after two years of working together. The briefing went smoothly, subteams were formed quickly, and the work began with skill and purpose. Any one of the twenty-two could deftly chair a subteam, soliciting ideas from all members of the group, assigning tasks, directing plans, creating consensus. They dispersed to observe classes, returned to the midday briefing, settled into writing their reports, and went to the huge auditorium like a professional drill team—enthusiastic, competent, and confident. Speaking to their colleagues no longer frightens them; indeed, they looked forward to this opportunity to share their observations, make suggestions, and engage in the important work of strengthening schools.

Their reports made my heart sing. Among the commendations and suggestions were personal glimpses about shared students that forged bonds between the speakers and the listeners. One team member expressed delight that some of her struggling mathematics students from last year were excelling in advanced mathematics classes; and another, who has taught first grade for twenty years at Miami Park Elementary School, told the Central High teachers how gratifying it was for her to see her own students of twelve years ago preparing for their graduation. No trembling voices, no shaky knees, no lack of confidence, but rather, as one team member wrote in the year-end evaluation, "more pride and a greater sense of commitment."

How others view the teachers

When SUNRAYS started, all of the team members were viewed as successful teachers, and some were viewed as leaders in their own building. Two years later, they are viewed by their peers and administrators as strong instructional leaders—in their school, their region, and the entire district. An assistant principal shared her first impression of the team when she saw them in her building this year, the third year of the project: "I got the impression that these were a diverse group of people who know about effective schools and how a school should operate!"

On a more personal level, one of the principals described how her two SUNRAYS teachers are viewed by other teachers in the school: "Teachers are receptive to their coming in to teach a group, to help them plan. In the past, that wouldn't have been the case." Asked how she accounts for the difference, she elaborated:

They see that these are hard-working people; these are not people just giving lip service. They're there to serve. They'll take the most difficult children in a class and help them succeed. They'll go in and say, "What can I do for you, to assist you in working with your boys and girls?" They have gone the extra mile. "Let me go in and assist in the organization of that classroom." "Let me help you with the development of an interesting bulletin board." "Let me look at how you're organizing your files." Teachers recognized they are serious about their role and really started opening up to them. The SUNRAYS teachers know who they are. They know their role, and they're willing to do what it takes for the betterment of the entire school.

The point is echoed by another principal: "I see a level of confidence in them [the SUNRAYS teachers] that wasn't there before. B. . . . has blossomed. He's taken on the morning announcements; he asked to be student government sponsor; he set up a system of transportation for kids who stay after school. I mean, there's a leadership there that wasn't there before. If you want to know how other teachers see him, they elected him teacher of the year this year!" The other SUNRAYS teacher in the school is viewed by her peers as the "in-house writing expert."

Additional leadership roles

Asked what other leadership roles they have taken on since their involvement in SUNRAYS, team members responded with example after example of new responsibilities. Several had become grade-level chairpersons, two now chair their school-based management faculty councils, others regularly facilitate in-service workshops for teachers, and many have voluntarily initiated programs for students, teachers, and parents such as a brain bowl for middle and high school students, a buddy system for advanced students in the middle and high schools, a parent volunteer program, and a student of the month program.

Some of these teacher leaders serve the wider community as well. One, for instance, recently chaired the United Negro College Fund telethon for her sorority. She was named last month to serve on the Dade County Commission on the Status of Women, and she volunteered at the 1994 Summit of the Americas, held in Miami.

A Project RAISE "graduate" who just joined SUNRAYS this year sums it up: "I have more confidence to take the lead in projects at school and outside."

Leadership skills developed

What specific leadership skills were developed through SUN-RAYS? The ability to facilitate the work of a small or large team, either as a member or as a leader; to express opinions, even those that differ; to observe instruction without intimidating the observed teacher or distracting the students; to record observations in such a way that the response will be positive and constructive; to report teaching practices so that others can implement them; to express themselves clearly, listen carefully, reach consensus, and write reports that include divergent viewpoints; and to speak before adult audiences clearly, persuasively, and enthusiastically.

One of the teachers, from Van E. Blanton Elementary School, exemplifies the emergence of a strong leader. When SUNRAYS began, she was already recognized in her own school as a competent, helpful colleague. SUNRAYS team members warmed to her ready smile and open manner, and she was soon viewed by them, too, as an able guide. It was she who was called upon to lead the RAYS team on a site visit when Billy had to be elsewhere, and according to everyone involved, including the team members and the principal, she led the process with ease.

The teacher recalls her own transformation:

We were like neophytes. We were scared and didn't really know what we were looking for. So we developed indicators [of best teaching practices] to help us know what to look for. . . . We were peers communicating with peers to share with each other what we did best—also to let them know there's some connection within the feeder pattern. We could borrow from each other, grow from each other. I have grown so much that I feel I'm a *strategist*, that I can actually go into a classroom or into a group of educators and suggest prescriptions for improving students' weaknesses. I think that's what we got from visiting schools. You might have something that I don't have, and I see it's working, and I'm going to take it and put it into practice. That's what happened to me.

Teachers, paraprofessionals, and administrators are depending on me more and giving me more responsibilities in curriculum planning and designing. I'm helping to save some teachers who had little hope of succeeding. And we're using so many new techniques now. Most of our teachers have dropped the old traditional way, and now they are using more of the indicators that we published. . . . They're asking more questions, and sharing ideas. I see things in the classrooms now that I didn't see before.

When I come back from the SUNRAYS visits, they want to know, "What do you have that you can share?" because I've been sharing every day. . . . I don't know of any other thing we could have done in our feeder pattern that could have reached so many teachers and so many students all at the same time.

The assistant principal calls this teacher "an asset to the administrative staff who can get people to work together. She's got those organizational skills, good writing skills, good speaking ability, and interpersonal skills. She can get staff members to work together to complete a task."

The principal's role

This transformation did not occur overnight. It did not occur to the same extent in every team member. And it did not occur without the wholehearted support of principals. In fact, the growth in the teacher leaders can almost be gauged by the amount of interest, encouragement, and active support they received from their principals. One principal put it this way:

The principal's role has two perspectives. The first is with the feeder pattern, wherein you're working with your colleagues to see that there's cohesiveness in the instructional program, in case children move from one school to the next. It used to be that our schools were always in different places in the curriculum. Now children can fit right in with fewer problems, when they move from school to school.

The other perspective is the one within your school. Your staff understands that even though these are SUNRAYS teachers, they are teachers like all the rest. You have to be careful not to show favoritism. Others will be called on for other leadership roles. I make it a point to call on those who don't often go out and get involved.

This principal is clearly committed to developing leadership in all of her teachers, not just through SUNRAYS but through other avenues as well.

The same principal spoke of changes in her own role as a result of SUNRAYS: "My role as a principal has changed. When I confer with teachers now, formally or informally, the conference tends to be longer—we have more to say about best teaching practices, and I have found this to be very rewarding and rich."

Another principal comments, "My role is one of a facilitator. We're all professionals; we can work together. I can't do it all by myself. The AP [assistant principal] can't do it. We're *all* key members of the staff." That assertion is borne out time and again by the involvement of SUNRAYS teachers in staff development activities, grade-level planning sessions, individual support for their colleagues, and continual assistance in improving instruction.

The lead principal in the feeder pattern describes her responsibilities: "Mine is a double role, and it's very difficult. I have to see that my school is on track and also keep principals [in our feeder pattern] challenged—not as a supervisor but as a peer. I have to challenge these guys and gals to stay on their toes, to be sure their instructional programs are meeting the needs of the teachers and kids." She goes on to say, "My job is easier now, because the SUNRAYS teachers are leaders in the school. . . . I trust their competence."

Because they are comfortable not only with their own responsibilities but also with sharing power and influence, these principals play a key role in developing teacher leaders. They release the potential of their teachers by expressing confidence in them, by allowing them to take on important work beyond the classroom, and by supporting them as they do it.

Benefits

The benefits of SUNRAYS accrued to the teacher leaders who participated as team members, to other teachers in the eleven schools, to the principals, and to the students. Team members either continue to serve in the project or have moved into other leadership roles. In addition, their own teaching has been enriched. A social studies teacher at Central High wrote at the end of last year: "The ability to see other teachers using best practices has allowed me to enhance my own teaching. Going to elementary schools rekindled my sense of creativity and sparked a yearning for a new teaching style in my own classroom. . . . I plan on using much of what I learned from other teachers to help my students learn in a creative and exciting classroom environment." Another teacher, from an elementary school, put it this way in one of our sessions: "I figured if I was out telling other teachers how to do it better, I'd better be sure my own house was in order first!" She is modest—she had already been named her own school's teacher of the year—but her point rang true with other team members. They all feel that their own teaching has improved as a result of their SUNRAYS experience, partly because they recognize that they are viewed as models and partly because they have learned new techniques or refined existing strategies as a result of their observations. These teachers continue to grow beyond their own classrooms. One wrote, "The members of the SUNRAYS team were very motivating, and [they] inspired me to pursue higher goals in my own teaching career." Another completed her doctorate during the first year of SUNRAYS, moved to a school in another feeder pattern as a curriculum specialist, and is preparing to help that feeder pattern launch SUNRAYS.

Removing the isolation in which they taught and publicly celebrating their successes have proved to be the primary benefits for other teachers in the schools. One teacher told us after the visit, "Before today, the only time adults came to my room was for a required evaluation or to get something from me! This is the first time I can remember another adult coming into my classroom because they were *interested* in what I was doing." Another testimony to teachers' satisfaction at being observed was expressed by the journalism teacher at the high school. He had not expected to be observed, because his is an elective subject; but not only did team members come to his classes, they also told the rest of the faculty in detail about a successful activity he conducted with his students. This recognition of his work was still the subject of conversation months later, at Central High School's commencement exercises.

How did principals perceive SUNRAYS? One spoke for all of her peers when she wrote, in response to a request for a brief assessment of the influence of SUNRAYS on her school, "Teachers are more aware of what a literate learning environment involves. Classrooms are well stocked with trade books, magazines, newspapers for children to read at their comfort level. Teachers are displaying more children's work and fewer commercial products. Teachers are utilizing instructional centers as a vital part of their program. Cooperative learning strategies are more observable in the classrooms. Communication among staff members improves as they share best practices." Another wrote, "The feedback provided by the team has been motivating and helpful to the morale of the faculty. . . . The SUNRAYS team are viewed by peers as instructional leaders at Broadmoor." From a third principal came this response: "SUNRAYS has had a positive impact on the instructional program at Lakeview Elementary. Staff members look forward to the team's annual visit. This visit brings out the best in everyone. The suggestions and commendations are always welcomed. They go a long way to boost staff morale. The teacher participants have learned a lot and have always brought back pointers that have helped us in our program. This is the best program in Region III as far as staff development goes."

One of the SUNRAYS team members wrote that the most important thing about the project was that "we are all working for the same goal—to help children." The children in these eleven schools are the primary beneficiaries of this effort. During the two years of the project, their achievements have steadily grown. Last year, for example, standardized measures of student performance improved across the board, in reading, writing, and mathematics. While SUNRAYS is surely not solely responsible for those gains, it is clear from teachers' and administrators' comments that the project has played a leading role in improving classroom instruction, so it is fair to say that part of the improved student achievement is due to the efforts of the SUNRAYS teacher leaders.

Considerations for new implementations

Those who might consider implementing SUNRAYS in their own community of schools should know that the most essential prerequisite for success is commitment from leaders, both those who initiate and those who support the project. In our case, unconditional support was provided by the region superintendent, central office resource personnel, and the staff members of our teacher education center.

Leadership for the project also comes from the lead principal, who ensures that principals in the eleven schools communicate often and effectively. She uses regular meetings, a telephone tree, and frequent personal calls to maintain a focus on curriculum and instruction and to generate enthusiastic participation in feeder-pattern projects.

Reference has already been made to the key role that principals play; it is worth reinforcing. Casey's principal at West Little River Elementary School is a case in point. As Casey wrote, "She represents a stellar example of one who lends support to the very essence of the SUNRAYS project. She cultivates teachers as leaders and realizes how teachers in her school have the capacity and commitment to contribute beyond their classrooms. Realizing this, she encourages her potential teacher leaders to take on more responsibilities, more decision-making power, and motivates them to show initiative and willingness to experiment with new ideas. She does all this in a gentle and compelling manner."

Leadership is also shared with the assistant principals in participating schools. Along with the principals, they are active supervisors of the schools' instructional programs, and they regularly tap teachers' talents for leadership roles. They include teachers in the feeder pattern's curriculum council meetings, they select teachers for attending and presenting in-service activities, and they regularly draw on teachers as resources for one another. The assistant principals have worked closely with the SUNRAYS team members in their own schools, encouraging them to share what they have learned from neighboring schools and providing avenues for them to assist their peers.

Expectations for SUNRAYS

Adapters of this project have the advantage of knowing ahead of time some of the outcomes they might expect. Clearly, the project is successful in doing what it was designed to do: nurturing the growth of all teachers, improving the academic performance of students, and strengthening the bonds among schools. Beyond those successes, however, has been the surprising and gratifying development of teacher leaders, teachers who are now poised and ready to initiate projects on their own and to work for positive changes in their schools. Knowing this, adapters can consciously plan for teachers' development and thus hasten their growth. As we start anew with a second feeder pattern later this year, the first item on the agenda of the initial briefing will be a panel discussion by Casey and other SUNRAYS teachers, who will tell the new team members what this project has meant to them. We think their comments will launch the new project more successfully than anything else we could do. For leaders who want to improve instruction, celebrate good teaching, and develop teacher leaders, SUNRAYS may be the means for shedding light on a potential harvest of excellence.

Note: Billy and Casey have developed a SUNRAYS packet for potential adapters. It includes a project description; a list of participating schools, principals, and team members; this year's time line, the checklist of indicators of best practices, the schedule for site visits, directions to subteams, and forms for written reports and examples of best practices. Contact Dr. Billy F. Birnie, Dade County Public Schools, 1080 LaBaron Drive, Miami Springs, FL 33166, or call 305–882–1879.

BILLY F. BIRNIE *is regional director for instructional support in one of six regions in the Dade County Public Schools, Miami, Florida.*

CASEY LUSTGARTEN *is reading resource specialist teacher at West Little River Elementary School, Miami, Florida.*

*If teachers are to be leaders, their preparation as leaders must
be examined. The author, a university professor, contrasts
preparing teachers to be administrators with preparing teachers who do not wish to move into administration to be formal
and informal leaders in their schools. He asserts a need to
rethink the development of leadership, including making significant changes to educational administration programs at
universities. He concludes there is much to be done to find common ground in the appropriate preparation and support of all
leaders in schools.*

8

Finding common ground:
Teacher leaders and principals

Lee Teitel

I LEAD A DOUBLE LIFE. For the last six years, my "real job" has been
to teach in an educational administration program at a university.
I work with experienced teachers who wish to get prepared and cre-
dentialed to be principals or other administrators. But each year I
have also held one or more "side jobs"—facilitating action research,
mentoring institutes, peer coaching, helping school change initiatives. In these capacities I work with experienced teachers who are
interested in leading but most distinctly do not want to become
administrators. In fact, many of them have negative feelings toward
administrators.

Both groups of teachers are demographically similar: they typically are in their thirties and forties, with an average of fifteen years

NEW DIRECTIONS FOR SCHOOL LEADERSHIP, NO. 1, FALL 1996 ©JOSSEY-BASS PUBLISHERS of teaching experience. The readings and activities we do are often similar—both prospective administrators and teacher leaders might want to learn about organizational change or action research, for example. Yet the fundamental difference in their career direction and expectations leads to important differences in what goes on in our work together. Working with teacher leaders has informed what I do with prospective administrators in powerful ways, which I outline in this chapter. After a brief background introduction, the first part of the chapter examines the kind of issues teacher leaders bring to the workshops I conduct, how they compare to the issues brought by prospective administrators, and some strategies I have used that seem to increase my effectiveness in supporting teacher leaders. The second part of the chapter focuses on implications these experiences have had for me: implications for the preparation of teacher leaders and prospective administrators and, more broadly, for how I think about what it means to lead in schools.

My work with teacher leaders

My first sustained contact with teacher leaders was in 1992, as part of a leadership strand I facilitated for the Massachusetts Academy for Teachers. The academy, funded by the U.S. Department of Education, brought together 125 K–12 teachers from around the state for eight Saturday workshops during each of two academic years and for a two-week session during the intervening summer. The program focused on the renewal and enhancement of teachers' knowledge of five core academic disciplines, teaching practices and curricula, and leadership skills. Six leadership strands were offered: mentoring, teacher research, technology, policy, curriculum development, and managing and initiating change in schools (which I facilitated). The strands represented arenas in which participants had begun to initiate and implement changes at a variety of educational levels. Each participant had a different area of interest, but they were united in their desire to continue as classroom teachers and to have a greater impact on what was going on in their school. Most used the summer to develop action plans, frequently carving out new roles for themselves as teacher leaders in schools where there were precious few role models. They served as curriculum change agents, visionaries, and resources on instructional approaches they had tried in their classrooms. Each leadership strand met for six sessions over the summer and for three follow-up meetings in the fall and winter.

My experience with the Massachusetts Academy for Teaching had several profound effects on me as a teacher at my university and, more recently, as director of its educational administration program. It led to a variety of follow-up workshops and seminars with other teacher leaders—a year-long academy leadership program, several programs for mentor teachers, and two year-long action research projects with teachers documenting change in their Accelerated Schools program (a school reform effort that tries to offer an enriched curriculum to all students). Approaches to teaching that grew out of my interactions with teacher leaders in the less structured environment of these seminars have been infused into, and have transformed, my "regular" teaching at the university. Programmatic strategies that proved successful in working with the teacher leaders—the use of cohorts, for instance—have been incorporated into the design of our master's and doctoral programs. Furthermore, my understanding of the issues faced by teacher leaders has shaped the content as well as the processes of the educational administration program. The differences that emerge in working with teacher leaders have prompted me to rethink some of my assumptions about our principal preparation program. These differences are outlined below, followed by some of the impacts they have had on my thinking.

Issues teacher leaders bring to workshops

Teachers who choose to take leadership roles in their schools without leaving the classroom have little or no positional authority. Furthermore, since they have not been "anointed and appointed," as many teacher leaders have been in the past (Smylie and Denny, 1990), they deal with a higher level of ambiguity. Their lack of a formal sanction of their leadership efforts and of formal positional power has several side effects, influencing their relationships with those in authority and with their colleagues, how they collaborate with other teachers, and how they cope with opposition.

Sorting out relationships with those in positions of authority.   Many of the teacher leaders in these seminars express antagonism toward their principal, or at least a sense of disappointment over the lack of support they receive for their change initiatives. I often hear educational administration students, especially near the start of the program, express similar sentiments about poor principals they have known. (It seems that many teachers who go into administration do so despite their role models.) But although they are sometimes critical of the individuals, the administration students are usually more accepting of the structured role of the principal, because they generally believe they can do it better and because their coursework and practica usually give them a fuller understanding of the limits and pressures on the principal's position.

Neither of these factors comes into play for most of the teacher leadership group, however. Most of them have no desire to become a principal nor any opportunity or desire to more fully understand the principal's perspective. Their relationship to the power of authority is different. Even strong and self-confident teacher leaders appear to remain very aware of who is really the boss. An example of this emerged in a year-long action research seminar for teachers, documenting their Accelerated School's progress. As the year progressed, two of the teachers expressed increasing levels of concern when their data began to lead to conclusions that they thought the principal might object to. As one put it, "She'll kill us if we put that in the report!" The discussion that followed among the other twenty teachers included suggestions about how to approach the principal, but the teachers always maintained a grudging fear of the principal's potential powers of retribution. Would-be principals can be just as sensitive to the power of authority, but they also know that one day they will have that positional power.

Sorting out attitudes toward teachers who are less willing to change.   Participants in the teacher leadership workshops often express goals such as "reenergizing fellow teachers" or "developing approaches to help turn other teachers into 'dreamers.'" Although some participants objected to the phraseology, many listed "waking up the deadbeats" as one of their goals—that is, energizing those on their faculty whom they perceive as resistors to change.

Would-be administrators also focus on resistors. However, if moral leadership, simple persuasion, or attempts to cajole teachers to do something are unsuccessful, resorting to blunt power is implicitly, and sometimes explicitly, a part of the repertoire for potential principals. Even though many prospective principals prefer not to rely on positional power, it remains an option. This is rarely a choice for teacher leaders, however. The only way they could wield power would be to ask their principal to do it for them, something most would prefer not to do.

Developing skills in approaching and involving others. At one level this means developing the oral and written skills needed to organize and present one's ideas to colleagues and administrators. At another it means developing strategies for initiating or maintaining a change and sorting out whom to talk to and when and how. Because teacher leaders have no positional power, they are particularly interested in figuring out ways to motivate others in a "kindly" way or, as one teacher put it, in "how to be a leader without intimidating people." Central to the task for those involved in the Accelerated Schools documentation efforts, for instance, has been developing and implementing strategies for engaging colleagues and getting shared ownership of the effort.

Sorting out what leadership and involvement of colleagues actually means. In workshop sessions and role plays, issues emerge concerning leadership, ownership, and delegation of tasks in change efforts. As we unpack the notion of what it means to develop shared ownership of a change effort, we notice how different it is from delegating tasks to others. Many of the teacher leaders I have worked with have some unexplored ambivalence about really sharing decision making with others, preferring to involve others through the delegation of tasks. This has led to fascinating discussions of what joint ownership of a change process looks like. For prospective principals, these kinds of conversations have different nuances, since their role responsibilities and account-ability will usually be seen as different.

Coping with a sense of personal isolation. Closely related to the last two issues are what participants express as their hope of getting past the "shining star" syndrome—of being seen as the one teacher who is always ready to take on a new project, in contrast to the rest of the faculty, who are viewed as "entrenched" or "burned out." When we talked at one session about the importance of develop-ing a vision, one teacher asked plaintively, "Aren't visionaries always alone—off in the desert somewhere?" The need for support seemed important to most, especially as they realized they were not just talking about skills in how to share ideas and engage others in making change but were also struggling against school norms that tell teachers to close their classroom doors and not "meddle" in the affairs of other teachers.

On the other hand, prospective principals, although not pleased about it, often express the expectation that it will be "lonely at the top." In making a career change, they anticipate some degree of isolation; for teacher leaders there is no analogous career change (with increase in pay, and concomitant change in expectations) to explain or offset the isolation.

Finding the courage and stamina to persist. A special educa-tion teacher who hoped to change the attitudes and approaches of regular education teachers in her school expressed the sentiments of many when she asked, "Do I have the courage to do this?" The question was not rhetorical but expressed a real concern of many in the group about the possible consequences of leadership—dis-approval from colleagues and retaliation from the administration. Related to this was the (often unstated) question of how much responsibility a teacher has to take outside her classroom to try to improve her school. A belief in a vision and the importance of act-ing on it guides most of these teacher leaders, but there remains a strong temptation to close that classroom door and avoid poten-tially difficult issues with other teachers or administrators who may be unsupportive or threatened.

Prospective principals need this courage to persist as well, but it has a slightly different meaning for them. Once she becomes a principal, a former teacher cannot casually back away from leadership and "close the classroom door." Although some principals choose to leave the principalship to return to teaching, it is quite rare. More often the issue for principals is retaining vision and purpose in the face of opposition. In fact, teacher leaders who have "crossed over" and enrolled in my regular educational administration courses have challenged the prospective principals there, asking them why they think they will be different, challenging them to show why, after a few years in office, they will not revert to the managerial roles that most principals appear to take.

Lessons learned in working with teacher leaders

There are several approaches that seem to work well with teacher leaders. For me, many of them evolved during that first Massachusetts Academy leadership strand. In a paper I wrote shortly after that program concluded (Teitel, 1993), I described six approaches that I felt were key to whatever success we had attained. Those approaches are described below, followed by a description of the impact they had on my "real" job of teaching educational administration as well as on my continued work with teacher leaders.

The seminar worked because the teachers chose to be there. This leadership strand, along with the other five offered by the academy, was set up in response to the wishes of the participants. Once the strands were determined, the teachers got short descriptions of each and then chose one; if they did not like it, they switched to another strand.

The program worked because the teachers were genuinely engaged in shaping its progress, refining it as we went. Each session (except the first) was planned collaboratively. The overall framework was set by the group as a whole, and a volunteer subgroup of about seven or eight of us met a half hour before each session to develop the actual agenda for the day. Overall, the academy functioned similarly, with strong input by the teachers into virtually every decision.

Ironically, the seminar worked better because I didn't know too much about the topic. If I knew more of the literature on change—if I were a real "expert"—I might have felt compelled to share my "expertise." In retrospect, it would have been a real loss if I had tried to make the seminar more teacher-centered and content-driven (although I doubt the teachers would have allowed me to do so).

It worked because the teachers were treated with respect. Every aspect of the way the academy was organized treated teachers as important professionals who could and should help determine the direction of their professional development. Good food, stipends for participating, a variety of stimulating and fun activities characterized the academy overall and created the context for this particular seminar. Within the group, teachers were identified from the first day as experts, and we shared our expertise throughout.

It worked because there was time for bonding (over the summer) as well as some continuity over the school year. Because they were actively engaged in ongoing projects, the teachers could provide concrete examples of support for one another and make the overall experience of looking together at managing and initiating change much more meaningful.

Finally, the seminar worked because it engaged people in a powerful, supportive group process. We created a supportive learning community that provided an alternative to the traditional framework that tells teachers to close the classroom door and leave the running of the school to others. A final anecdote illustrates this. A few weeks after the last change strand meeting, at the academy's closing ceremony, I ran into one of the quieter, more reserved members of the seminar. I had assumed that she had not found the seminar highly rewarding, but she excitedly told me about something that had just happened in her school. She described how she had spoken up at a faculty meeting to promote an activity that she thought might help heal the deep racial divisions in her school. She spoke of her decision to take what she knew would be an unpopular stand: "I knew there would be dead silence, or the other teachers would roll their eyes and start talking about me behind my back.

But I thought about you and the group and what we have been talking about here all year and I knew I had to do it."

Implications: successful steps and worrisome doubts

These lessons about the importance of choice, participatory planning, joint inquiry, respect, bonding, and ongoing support networks have been powerful ones for me. Not only have they become touchstones in my subsequent work on action research documentation, peer coaching, mentoring, and other teacher leadership techniques, they have shaped my teaching and my thinking about the preparation of administrators in important ways. A few months after completing the Massachusetts Academy change strand, I was asked, along with Karen O'Connor, director of the academy, to reflect on the implications that working with teacher leaders might have on the preparation of principals. In the article we wrote for the Danforth Principal Preparation Network newsletter (Teitel and O'Connor, 1993), we pointed to several ways in which principal preparation programs could combine the best features of the academy in format and delivery, and we discussed how they should be informed by an understanding of the importance of the emerging role of teacher leader. We proposed that prospective administrators

- Develop strong cohorts that allow for caring, supportive relationships
- Be involved, as an integral part of their program, in sustained efforts to bring about change in their schools
- Have available to them, after the completion of the program, ongoing support networks, so new principals can continue to learn on the job and get the benefit of peer support

Furthermore, we argued that the content of programs should shift so that principals

- Learn to see teacher leaders not as pesky troublemakers to be "managed" but as valuable resources to be nurtured for school improvement
- Learn what kind of professional development programs support and foster the growth of teacher leadership, and, moreover, learn to model the role of continuing learners
- Learn what they can do to create school norms that encourage innovation and risk taking

When I look back to the suggestion list we generated several years ago, I can see we have made some steady progress. The Educational Administration program at the University of Massachusetts, Boston, just started admitting students in cohorts that travel through the two-year sequence together. Students take a required organizational change course that has them work as change agents in their own schools; this is used as a basis for teaching theory and practice. We encourage them to consciously see themselves as unsanctioned teacher leaders and to reflect on their school and its change process from that vantage point. Throughout the courses and the practicum, we focus on metacognition and their own learning about how they as teachers and experienced professionals learn best. We have done ropes courses and trust-building activities as ways to talk about risk taking for themselves and in their teacher roles. We have planned, but not yet implemented, an alumni support network.

Furthermore, the university has recently begun a doctoral program on leadership in urban schools that is specifically not just an administrative preparation program. Instead it includes active teacher leaders who want to develop and use leadership skills without leaving the classroom. Although many of these innovations are too new to evaluate, I am cautiously optimistic that we are moving in a direction that will prepare our graduates to have a broader view of school leadership and the knowledge, skills, and beliefs to work more effectively with teacher leaders.

So much for the good news.

Remaining challenges

Even as I am in the midst of this exciting transformation of teaching and learning about new approaches to leadership; even as I feel personally pleased with the progress my university has made in rethinking its school leadership programs, I have several nagging doubts. I see four interwoven challenges concerning the emerging nature of school leadership and how teachers and administrators can be best prepared and supported for their roles in it.

Finding common ground

While it is fine to talk about collaborative, participatory approaches to leadership in theory, there is still a great deal of work to do in defining, in a real-world context, what the common ground between teachers and administrators is. In most schools there is a such a strong us-them split that "establishing a collaborative culture" would be less than trivial. School leadership that embraces and includes teachers as active participants requires changes in fundamental conceptions, role definitions, and attitudes. For example, until recently I have assumed that part of the function of a principal preparation program is to socialize teachers into being ready and willing to assume a different role in schools—to shed, as Ackerman (1991) puts it, the student's "teacher self" and assume the role and perspective of an administrator. In a sense this involves crossing, in the parlance of many a teachers' lounge, the border from "us" to "them." I find myself wondering more and more how we can get away from the either-or dichotomy and find a common ground that creates a different kind of role for principals and teachers that is neither "us" nor "them."

Identifying appropriate knowledge and skill development

In addition to changes in culture and attitude, there are new sets of skills and knowledge needed by teachers and administrators. Teachers need skills that formerly only principals had: budgeting, staff development, evaluation, and so on. Teachers and principals need to add to their knowledge and skills in developing partnerships, creating communities, dealing with the change process, working with diverse stakeholders, conducting research, evaluating programs, and supporting the development of others. On top of this, teacher leaders need to develop additional skills in maintaining their relationships with their colleagues (Little and McLaughlin, 1993).

As a result of my "dual life" it is clear to me that, just as many traditionally trained principals will have difficulties working effectively with teacher leaders, many, if not most, teachers are not well prepared by their pre-service or in-service training or experience for schoolwide leadership roles. It is equally clear to me that developing and delivering this knowledge and these skills cannot be the purview of any one school, school district, college, or department of education, or any other sole in-service or pre-service provider. Providing preparation and support for teachers and administrators in this context of redefined leadership roles will require an unprecedented level of collaboration—collaboration between schools and universities; within school districts, among schools and between schools and school districts; and within universities, between departments of teaching and administrative preparation and between colleges of education and colleges of arts and sciences.

Finding the right scale

Assuming that common ground can be defined and clear definitions of what teachers and administrators should know or do can be clearly delineated, the scale of bringing about these changes is enormous. It is not just a question of trying to influence all pre-service and in-service principals—a daunting enough task—but of reaching all present and future teachers as well. The current reform movements ask classroom teachers to take on significant new leadership roles that are qualitatively different from earlier models, where teacher leadership was an add-on position involving a handful of individuals who were "appointed and anointed" (Smylie and Denny, 1990). At work is nothing less than a redefinition of what it means to be a teacher: indeed, two teacher leaders from Brookline, Massachusetts, have proposed that the National Policy Board for Professional Teaching Standards include a sixth "proposition" defining standards for what teachers should know and be able to do: "Teachers are leaders who reform their work, facilitate the development of others, and have influence in domains outside the classroom" (Troen and Boles, 1994, p. 14).

Even if it were simple to define and develop a knowledge and skill base appropriate for pre-service and in-service development of teachers and principals, the logistics of doing so are daunting, especially in tight financial times. Who will provide professional development for experienced educators? Who will pay for it? While the costs of becoming an administrator are usually borne by the individuals themselves, this is not the case for in-service principals or most experienced teachers. Programs like the Massachusetts Academy for Teachers provide wonderful experiences for teachers, but they are hard to institutionalize once external funding runs out.

Achieving critical mass

Most leadership development programs—all the ones I have been involved with—focus on the individual. Whether they are teacher leaders or prospective administrators, the individuals I work with will almost inevitably be isolated when they return to what are generally contexts characterized by more traditional notions of school leadership. The isolation they are likely to face in their own school speaks to the need (mentioned earlier) for ongoing support networks, but it also speaks to the challenge in fostering change without a critical mass to back you up. The lone, heroic change agent is a slow and inefficient approach to changing leadership paradigms in schools, and it puts substantial stress on the teacher leader. Although some of the programs I have been involved with have made adjustments to reduce isolation, like enlisting pairs of teachers to become action researchers in the Accelerated Schools network or developing team-based leadership projects in the Massachusetts Academy for Teachers follow-up program, these are minor adjustments that are, at best, palliatives. Imagine, by contrast, how different it would be for teachers conducting action research to report findings that might be seen as critical by the principal at a school whose culture already embraces collaborative decision making and genuine inquiry.

Pre-service teachers and administrators can face the same issues in their first jobs, where strong hierarchical cultures and norms push back innovative educators and reinforce traditional roles and expectations. Issues of critical mass cut both ways: often schools have developed collaborative leadership models that cannot be properly supported by the traditional in-service programs provided by their local colleges and universities, or they run into obstacles from their districts because new models of shared decision making upset the status quo.

Conclusion

Although I am excited about the teaching and learning that has been inspired by my work with teacher leaders, I have to conclude that there is still a great deal to be done and that most of it cannot be done by any one program. Although I have been personally very fulfilled by my opportunities to work with teachers seeking formal and informal leadership roles, I have come increasingly to realize the importance of going beyond individual steps toward coherent, interinstitutional collaborative approaches to rethinking leadership, leadership preparation, and support.

I see now that those of us in education and administration programs need to look for ways to cross the boundaries between us, to look at the common core of understanding about leadership and organizations that is relevant to both teachers and administrators. We need to look at how processes within education and administration departments model and reinforce the status quo, and we need to break down the patterns that compartmentalize in-service and pre-service programs, teacher preparation and administrator preparation, theory and practice. Schools, school districts, colleges of education, and colleges of liberal arts cannot all develop and support new leadership paradigms independently.

The most promising places where these barriers are being crossed and common ground between teachers and administrators is being defined are in professional development schools, described more fully in Chapter Three. Professional development schools bridge the gap between school and college and between theory and practice, and they provide opportunities for the ongoing professional development of all the educators involved. They place new demands on formal leaders, and they provide a myriad of opportunities for other teacher leadership. They also have great potential to induct new educators into the profession in ways that recognize and prepare them for different norms of collaboration and leadership.

The challenges outlined above to finding common ground between teacher leaders and administrators are very real. As Barth puts it, "Coalition-building and the replacement of competitive relationships with collegial ones does not occur easily, let alone naturally. Schoolpeople need skills, insight, and vision that will equip them to assume responsibility for their schools. Such tools are seldom won through experience as classroom teachers or principals, or in courses of schools of education" (1990, p. 11). We need to work together in schools, colleges and universities, school districts, and communities to find that common ground and to provide preparation and support, in context, to all those who are trying to embrace the greater leadership role of teachers in schools.

References

Ackerman, R. "Portraits of Practicum Life: Toward an Understanding of Field Experience for Aspiring Principals." Paper presented at the annual meeting of the American Educational Research Association, Chicago, April 1991.

Barth, R. *Improving Schools from Within: Teachers, Parents, and Principals Can Make the Difference.* San Francisco: Jossey-Bass, 1990.

Little, J. W., and McLaughlin, M. (eds.). *Teachers' Work: Individuals, Colleagues and Contexts.* New York: Teachers College Press, 1993.

Smylie, M., and Denny, J. "Teacher Leadership: Tensions and Ambiguities in Organizational Perspective." *Educational Administration Quarterly*, 1990, 26(3), 235–259.

Teitel, L. "Teachers as Leaders in Managing and Initiating Change." Paper presented at the Annual Meeting of the American Educational Research Association, Atlanta, Georgia, April 15, 1993.

Teitel, L., and O'Connor, K. "Teachers as Leaders: Implications for the Preparation of Principals." *CONNECTIONS! Newsletter of the Danforth Principal Preparation Network*, 1993, 2(1), 5.

Troen, V., and Boles, K. "The Case for Including Teacher Leadership as a Criterion for National Board Certification: Introducing Proposition Six." Discussion paper prepared for the Education Policy and Reform Working Group of the National Policy Board for Professional Teaching Standards, 1994.

LEE TEITEL *is associate professor in the Education Administration Department at the University of Massachusetts, Boston.*

Index